IF DEAD COWS
COULD TALK

IF DEAD COWS COULD TALK

NANCY BELLVILLE

AB PUBLISHING, INC.

Printed by
AB Publishing, Inc.
3039 S. Bagley Rd.
Ithaca, MI 48847

DEDICATION

This book is dedicated to our children, Dawn, Lori, Andrea, Kevin, and Kay, who helped us build our farm and, when things turned sour, stood behind us. Without their help over the years, Nansue Farms could not have grown and developed into the successful farm it was until 1998. I'd also like to dedicate this story to the relatives and friends whose support made our survival possible. Thank you to all of you.

Our story is the story of all the farmers who suffered from stray voltage. Each family has gone through the same situations we did but cannot talk about their particular experience for legal reasons. We dedicate this book to them also.

God led us down this road and kept us safe while we endured the roller coaster ride this story became. We thank Him for the strength to hang on.

CHAPTER 1

We all mark our life's journey by milestones such as weddings, the birth of a child, death of a loved one, or by national events: President Kennedy's death, the Challenger explosion, or the tragedy of September 11, 2001. However, on the Bellville farm, December 10, 1998, marks the date for the beginning of the mysterious downfall of a thriving farm operation.

My name is Nancy Bellville. I was born in Chicago; my parents, Ernest and Ila Mae Tripp, had moved there after W.W.II to go to music school on the GI bill. Both had served in the War, my Dad overseas in the Army, my Mom as a WAVE in Washington D.C. My Dad worked as a Security Guard at National Argonne, the laboratory where the Atom bomb was developed.

According to the news story, the time was February, 1951. The Cold War with Russia was heating up. China was lost to Communism. Atomic spies were being rounded up by the score. In addition, a young new shark named Paul Harvey had just been caught scaling the security fence at the Atomic Energy Commission's Argonne National Laboratory.

Harvey often used his radio broadcasts to criticize what he perceived to be poor security throughout the federal government. He found an opportunity for action when an Argonne guard and switchboard operator, Charles Rogel, reported lax security at the site to Harvey's friend, Representative Fred Busbey. As Harvey scaled the ten-foot fence, his winter overcoat caught in the barbed wire at the top. While he was trying to extricate himself, a jeep patrol found and detained him.

My Dad was second in command of the Security at Argonne. He was called in early that morning to question Paul Harvey. Disgusted with the whole incident, my Dad resigned and the later

investigation would prove security was at its best the morning
Paul Harvey was caught.

Having been a guard at National Argonne, my Dad applied for
a job with the US Border Guard. He was all set to go work for
them, but they told him he would have to leave his family at a
moment's notice to go on assignment and could not say where he
would be going. We would also move a lot. He decided since I was
just starting school, moving around would not be a good thing for
me. Moreover, he could not just go to work, be sent on assignment
and not be able to tell us where, when or if he would return.

Therefore, he applied for a job with Michigan State
University as a security guard. But the only housing available was
over the pig barn. Had there been housing anywhere else I would
have grown up in East Lansing, but he could not put us over the
pig barn. We did move back to Michigan where my parents had
grown up in the Saginaw Valley.

Dad started looking for a farm; he had grown up on a farm.
When I was five years old, they found one they could afford in a
little town called Prescott. Growing up in a small town is
wonderful. At that time, you knew everyone for miles around and
never had to lock your doors. As kids we played outdoors, rode
our bikes down the road and no one worried about us for hours.
We made up our own games and had a ball with life. However,
what I remember of Chicago is smog, and the water tasted like
fish. Funny the things you remember at five years of age. The
only toy I remember is an elephant that walked when you pulled
it, but it did not move with us. I've missed it for years.

We became involved in the community. My Dad with his
music background was a natural addition to the Minstrel Shows
that Prescott, Whittemore and West Branch held each year. He
was a comedian at heart. He would end up being in charge of
Prescott's show and would participate in the other shows. In one
show at Whittemore, he would impersonate Gene Sheldon, a
popular TV personality at that time, who never spoke but played
a banjo. In my dad's version, he would come out on stage to
perform and as he walked across the stage, he would almost trip
and fall. The MC would of course rush forward and warn him to
be careful. He would then play a banjo tune and then as he left the

stage, he would almost trip again. Later during the show it would be his turn again, and once again he would pull the banjo out in a box. This time he would not trip and he would look at the audience with a big smile on his face. As he turned to walk to the box to get his banjo, he would stumble and fall on the box breaking the banjo. The audience roared.

My dad always had a sense of humor and was happiest making people laugh. Music was his life, and he and my mom would have a dance band for many years, but it was the comedy that always drew him back.

While in the army, the guys called him "Wilful Stumble" because his last name was Tripp. While in Chicago, he had an artist draw what "Wilful Stumble" would look like. Dad wore a beat up old hat, red long underwear, big denim jeans held out at the waist by a wire run through the waistband and big rubber bare feet. It was an outfit he had made in Chicago. He used it as part of the Minstrel and Talent Shows with a comedy routine along with his one-man band called a "Whatzit".

Dad would not only perform at the Fairs in the community, but was a big hit at the nursing homes and at his grandkids' schools. He would later realize his dream of being on "HEE HAW", when they showcased comedy acts from the Fanfare held each year in Nashville. As comedy was my dad's passion, he had come to Prescott to farm with the same passion.

We had a small farm, but my Dad was ahead of his time. He put in one of the first milking parlors in the stanchion barn and built one of the first free stall barns in Michigan. Cows had always been tied up in stanchion barns; free stall barns allowed the cows to be loose and choose which stall they could walk into and lie down.

After contacting Michigan State University about an article on free stall barns, he sent to the state of Washington for the plans, as Michigan State University (MSU) determined our climate was too cold to house cows in an open barn. We have had such a laugh over the years about that, as today we put a roof over the barn and have the entire walls open most of the year.

After graduating in 1965, I married my husband Brian. His sister Ann was in my class in high school. I spent several nights at her house and that was when I met her brother Brian.

Brian was working the family farm and we had a lot in common. I knew how to drive a tractor and milk cows so he didn't have to teach me much. It was different going from a milking parlor where you stand in a pit and the cows are in front of you to having to go in between each animal and bend down and put the milkers on them. The cows are so big and they like to squeeze you. I never did get comfortable milking that way.

MSU would always play a big role in our lives. Brian had graduated from the MSU two-year short course, as it was known then. This is a very intense study of farming procedures. The courses are designed to be available for students to study in the fall and winter when the farm work is not as intense, as in planting and harvesting seasons. The first few months after we were married we attended our first of many seminars that MSU would put on in the area. This meeting was on fertility. Being the only woman there was more embarrassing for the professors than for me. Most women back then stayed home. That was before the days of Women's Lib. Most farm women worked along side their husbands and shared the work load. Once we went to a meeting and the professor went around the room to find out what the women helped with on the farm. When he got to me I said, "I milk cows, feed calves, help with the fieldwork and do the book keeping." He wanted to know what my husband did. I said, "He managed." The professor said, "Anyone who could get out of that much work was a darn good manager." We laughed about that for a long time. Brian had his responsibilities and I had mine.

We came to farm with my parents in 1966. The farm as we came to it consisted of two barns, forty cows and young cattle. My parents had named all of the animals from the beginning and the registered females had the prefix of NANSUE (NAN for me, Nancy, and the SUE for my sister Susan). They had also added some more land. They named the pieces of property after whoever we had purchased it from so at this time they had three properties: the home farm, Moggs and the King place. We kept the Nansue name for our registered animals and would call our farm Nansue Farms when we went on our own in 1968.

CHAPTER 2

We would start the expansion process with a silo in 1966. We would also add 120 acres of our own. We bought the farm across the road to the North and it would become known as Carl's. We were by ourselves now. We both helped with chores and then would go to the field.

One day I was dragging (using a piece of equipment that leveled the dirt) and turned too short and caught the drags on the wheel. Brian had to come help me get them back down. I had my choice, I could go milk by myself, or I could keep dragging as Brian had always milked before. I chose the lesser of the two evils. I left him to drag and I milked.

Milking became my job and the cows my responsibility. The land, machinery, maintenance, feeding, and breeding the cows became Brian's responsibility. And so our partnership was formed. By the way, Brian put a chain on the tongue of the drag, so that I could turn without catching the drag on the wheel of the tractor. I never did get out of fieldwork.

The days ran pretty much the same. Get up do chores, go to the field, do chores, eat, sleep, and start all over again. By 1972, we were building a milking parlor; we were adding cows and fast outgrowing the old barn. We were so busy building the parlor that when asked what she wanted for Christmas, Lori age three, only wanted a Christmas tree. We finally got it up Christmas Eve.

We had added a couple of silos and by 1978, we added another barn after the existing barn collapsed, a free stall barn, tool shed, two more silos and additions on the barn. In 1992 we built a calf barn and a heifer barn. We were adding land at the same time.

Each piece of land seemed to set and wait for us to be able to afford to add it. One piece, Webster's, would wait for eight years, just setting vacant. The people who owned it raced horses, so they were not there very much. As a kid growing up, I remember they had a goat. I hated that goat because he would chase you and I was afraid of him. My sister Susie loved that goat. She went over and got him one day as he always ran loose. She brought him home and that goat chased me up the straw stack in the barn. This is where my folks would find me, screaming my head off. I hated that goat.

The next piece would be farther down the road. Brian has always been a good steward of the land. When we bought a piece, we cleaned out the fencerows and got rid of any obstructions in the way like trees. So we always had an open clear field to work in. Besides, if there were no trees or fences, his wife couldn't hook the drag on them. It is called self-preservation and fewer repairs. As one of the neighbors asked over the fence one day, "Does your husband appreciate all the work you do?" I said, "No, but you can tell him he should the next time you see him."

We have always shared everything—the good and the bad. Our last piece of property would come from that neighbor. He owned the farm together with his aunt. He was sixty-seven years old and his hips were bothering him. His aunt was eighty-seven. Brian had teased him that if he ever decided to sell, let us know.

One day he came and wanted to know if we wanted to buy it. It was so hard for his aunt to sign her name to the purchase agreement. I would not fully appreciate her feelings until fifteen years later when we had to sell a piece of that land. That piece of land would give us the cushion we needed. In a good year, it allowed us to have extra crops to sell and in a bad year, it gave us enough feed to get us through.

Finally, in 1996 our building process was complete with the addition of one final barn to house our dry cows (cows waiting to have babies) and a total of 740 acres of land. I could stand in our dining room, look out the sliding glass doors, and see our property to the North. We owned all of a section except forty acres. It is a beautiful piece of ground. The fields are clear and blend in with each other, from the hay on one side, to the corn in the center, and the soybeans on the other side. To watch each crop grow and to know the hard work that made it so beautiful only we can appreciate and only could have accomplished this monumental task with the help of our children and God.

By 1986, we had five children: Dawn, Lori, Andrea, Kevin, and Kaylene. Life was busy but the kids all pitched in and helped with chores. Dawn, the oldest, was always the boss. She was always at your elbow. At the age of three, she helped her Dad tear the combine engine apart. He worked and she got grease all over herself. She was so proud of helping him, although it was her birthday, and everyone in the family was coming for cake and ice cream. What a mess she was to clean up.

Dawn was there when they installed the feeders in the free stall barn and when Brian went fishing the next day and I could not get the feeder to switch sides, she was the one who told me the rope was caught on a peg that stuck up. She was six at the time, but she told me to come with her, and she would show me what to do. I asked her how she knew what to do and she said she had watched the day before and it had caught then and that was what they did for it to switch.

Lori was my cleaner; she baked and kept the house clean along with helping with outside chores, field work, and weeding my flowers and the garden. She was our runner, too. She still holds the high school record for the fastest time in the mile in track.

Andrea fed calves and milked the cows along with field work. When Kay was born, it would be Andrea's job to baby-sit. Kay is eight years younger than our youngest one, Kevin. At breakfast when the days task were passed out, a little voice would pipe up and say, "Who's watching me?" That was Kay.

Kay was my most patient one. She went to the barn right after she was born and slept in a bassinet in the office. She would go to sleep when the milkers started and not wake up until they shut off. She stayed in the bassinet until she was eleven months old, and I walked in one day and she was sitting on the desk. It was time now for the playpen; then she would sleep until chores were done. She would ride with us in the tractor and make a bed. One day as we plowed she said, "Where are the white birds?" It took me a while to realize she meant the gulls that are always around when you work a field.

Kevin was our mechanic. He learned to repair things because he had all of the women to work with and, if something broke and his Dad was out in the field, we ran for Kevin. He also felt it was his right to pick on Kay as the girls had picked on him.

It was not all work. Brian took each of the kids except Kay fishing. She says she does not want to go and eat fish all the time. We had a lot of fun times, too. Being together and sharing the day to day routine did get trying at times, but it also gave us stories to tell when we get together. I would like to tell our kids how much we appreciate all the hard work they did helping us build the farm. Thank you.

Farming is a way of life, but it does not come with eight hour days and weekends off. Dairy farming especially is hard; it is 365 days a year. For all of those years, I knew that at quarter to five each morning, I would be on my way to the barn to milk and we did not quit until after dark.

Over the years, we have spent a lot of time with our kids, even if it was picking rocks and clearing fence rows. Some of our best discussions were held during milking. No one interrupts you for a couple of hours, but Kevin never did convince me to buy him a new truck.

As we added land, one of the jobs that had to be done was pick stones, one of our favorite jobs. One time Dawn told a guy who was helping us and had pitched a rock over the fence on the neighbor's property that he might as well go pick the rock back up because her dad would probably buy that property next year, and he'd have to pick the rock up then. It was a lot of work but after picking rocks off a new property one year, the kids got a swimming pool for their efforts. Hard work never hurts any one and we all shared in it.

On the weekends or during the summer breakfast was when the day's tasks were handed out. It teaches responsibility, but I wondered if the kids realize the lessons we tried to teach them or whether it was just work to them.

When filling out a form for FFA, Future Farmers Association, a question was asked: What had living on a farm taught them? Lori replied that she had learned that when you are given a job to do, finish it because there might not be someone there to finish it for you.

Life on a farm has many lessons; one of them is that life on a farm always depends on the weather. Plans are made around the weather. If it rained all week and the weekend ended up nice, there might be work to do and not play time. This caused some disappointments when we had to postpone an activity to bale hay.

Brian and I would learn early on that one day can make a difference in whether you have enough feed to winter on or not. One year it was a wet fall and we could not get into the fields. We had harvested enough feed for a while, but not enough to get us through until spring. It finally froze one day in February. It sleeted all day, was really a miserable day, but the ground was frozen enough so we could chop. We harvested enough feed to hold us the rest of the winter. The next day it thawed out again, and we could not get more feed until spring. So we learned not to let a good day go by. You don't always get another one. That did not always set well with the kids.

My son once said he was going to get a job that did not depend on the weather. He did. Now he is a Mechanical Engineer. Lori implements computer programs. Andrea works for Mott Foods as an ingredient buyer. Kay is a freshman at MSU and Dawn married a farmer and has four children. All of them graduated from MSU. Kay was three years old before we could convince her there were other colors besides green and white. One of the kids was at college most of the time when she was growing up, but they came home to help when they could.

Farm life has its ups and downs, but the rewards come from the simple things like the smell of fresh mown hay or watching a new born calf nurse from its mother, or walking through a field of corn. Because it is your responsibility to care for the animals, a bond is formed between you and those creatures placed in your care; each of them has their own personality. To watch the seeds spout and come to life gives you a satisfaction. You can see your accomplishments.

There is an art and craftsmanship in keeping up machinery and using innovative farming techniques. Good feelings come from work done and done well. Farm life can also take its toll on the people on the farm. It can be all consuming. Farmers can't just leave the business at the office. The office is out their back door or around the corner.

Many become workaholics. Farm work is never finished, but with it comes a companionship. The hours we spent with our kids were more than some parents get by going to the office and having to place their kids in child care. The three hours we spent milking were three hours we caught up on things that happened at school or whatever was going on in their lives. As a kid growing up, milking with my Dad was the some of the happiest times I remember. We played games of who could name that tune. My sister and I got pretty good at it, but if we got stuck, we could always find an excuse to go to the house and ask my Mom. It was a lot of fun. As there were only my sister and I, we helped with all the chores and field work so I guess it was just natural that my kids would do the same thing on our farm. As farms have gotten larger it is harder for the kids to handle the larger equipment, and there isn't the companionship with the kids that there was when we or our kids were growing up. My grandkids that live on the farm all have things to do to help around the farm. Being responsible for the well-being of the animals teaches a lot of lessons that can't be learned elsewhere.

CHAPTER 3

Over the years we have met many people and made many friends. One friend in particular, Diane, would ask us for help, and she would live with us for about eight months when we needed some help milking cows while we did field work, so we got really close.

Years later, she would divorce and need a place for her babies (her herd of cows and her heifer calves).We asked our veterinarian for advice if we should move these animals on to our farm, as we were a closed herd not having brought outside animals into our herd for many years. He advised us to make sure they were vaccinated, which we did. Therefore, in November, 1995, we moved these animals on to our farm. They would stay for one year. In the process Diane was to oversee the cows, freeing me up to work in the field and not have to worry about stopping to do the milking. Diane would later decide to sell her cows, although we had them leased for one year.

Because we had the cows leased Diane could not remove them. Diane was responsible for milking the cows and, accidentally, some antibiotics got into the milk. That is absolutely not to happen. But somehow it happened twice. If it continued to happen, we would lose our license. The milk company purchasing our milk stated that if Diane continued to be on our farm they would not purchase our milk. We ended up with attorneys and letting Diane go and she could not come on our farm again.

Consequently, she would remove her young cattle, and the cows would leave at the end of the year. Our friendship would also end. We would later wonder if the favor was worth the results.

We had spent a lot of time with our herd of cows, choosing the best bulls to breed our animals, as we did not have a bull on the farm. My dad had sold the bull that was here when we came in 1952 and only once did Brian and I use a bull for our heifers. We had decided that with the kids, it just was not a safe situation. Too many farmers have been hurt or killed by their nice, friendly bulls. We have used AI, Artificial insemination, for over forty-five years.

Our cows were now starting to win awards at the Fairs from Reserve Grand Champion in 1981 to the top six junior animals. Dawn won Showman of Showman at the age of twelve. Kids from the different animal groups who had competed and won Showman in their class then competed for the overall Showman award. They would each show a cow, beef steer, pig and sheep. The one who did the best job of showing each animal (many kids had never handled that species before) was then selected for overall Showman of Showman.

In 1995, our local DHIA, Dairy Herd Improvement Association, award of top Junior two year old was awarded to one of our animals. The same year we would have another cow in the top ten junior two-year-olds. We would win this award two more times. 1996 we would win with cow #1370 and in 1999 we would again win with cow #1456. At this time, we would be the only herd to win this award three times. The many trophies that we and our kids won through the years for showing our dairy animals cover the tops of three file cabinets in our office and the ribbons line the walls. Along with the awards for the cows, Brian and I won the award given out by Soil Conservation District for Outstanding Conservation Farmer of the year in 1970 and again in 1985, also the Lifetime Dedication to Dairy Farming in 2000 from Michigan Milk Producers.

CHAPTER 4

As the years progressed, so did the community. In September of 1994, there would be a communication tower constructed about one quarter mile from our house. It would be used as a communication responder for Consumers Energy. This would become suspect several years later. As I have mentioned before we were progressive farmers, so as new ideas and equipment became available we might try something if it fit into our operation. One of those was a mat filled with rubber; our cows, like so many other farms, had laid on concrete platforms.

In 1995 we started having trouble with swollen hocks on some of our cows. Having found no medical reason for their condition, we decided to put mats on one side of the barn and see if the cows were more comfortable and the swollen hocks would go away. The mat did not seem to make any difference in the swollen hocks.

In 1997, we had noticed sores on the flanks of about six cows and heifers. The veterinarian lanced the sores, but the animal would die in a couple of weeks, without ever finding a cause.

We have always had goals. Over the years, we have usually met our goals ahead of time. In 1997, we had enough heifer calves born to increase our herd size by 1998 to 160 cows. We would have our short and intermediate debt paid off by 2005, two years ahead of schedule.

Then came 1998. In the fall we started to have more pervasive health issues with our herd: Too many Displaced Abomasums, twisted stomachs—cows have four stomachs—in our heifers and in cows six months in lactation; cows that had just had a hard time getting going after having their calves.

There was no reason why they should have any problems. We had only occasionally had any sick cows after they had their calves. Now it was getting to epidemic levels. We were getting very concerned. Ten cows quit giving milk, and we waited for them to gain weight so we could sell them. And we had more in pens waiting to die. Our veterinarian could not give a reason for this sudden occurrence.

We had not been able to increase our herd to 160 cows as planned, but even more alarming, we were now not able to maintain the 120 cows we had in 1995. We also had problems with milk yield, getting cows or heifers bred, seeing heats, a large number of stillborn calves and a large number of first-calf heifers with DA's, twisted stomachs. Our December DHIA report was dismal. We had freshened, animals having had babies, thirty-nine animals and removed forty-five animals during the year.

We attended a Farm Bureau Christmas party, and during this party a discussion came up about a farmer in the area who was having problems on his farm with his cows. He thought he had an electrical problem on his farm. I said to Brian, "Some of those symptoms sound like our cows. Do you think we have an electrical problem too?"

We did not know what to think. How could something like this happen in our area? Would the electrical company do something that would hurt our animals? Could that possibly be the cause of our cows being sick? We continued to have more sick cows, and our veterinarian, Dr. Tim Eyth, was as concerned and puzzled as we were. Dr. Eyth was more like a friend, having been with us since the early 1980's. He had watched our kids grow up.

One time he came out on a call while we were at lunch. Dawn, our oldest daughter, who was six at the time, said she would go out until we could get there.

She told the student with the vet to stay by the gate and Dr. Eyth to come with her and they would get the cow in the pen. She told him the cow had a temperature of 103.5 and he would know what that meant. By the time we got there, they had already started to check the cow out and Dr. Eyth said he wanted to take Dawn back to his office. He thought she would do a good job of running it for him. We laughed about that over the years.

Dr. Risley would join the practice in the mid 1980's. He would come out if it was his turn to be on call, but each one had his own clients and we were Dr. Eyth's.

My kids always played such an important role in the farm. They each had animals that were their own. Andrea at the age of six was determined; she had a calf that had developed a hay belly, when a calf eats too much hay and its belly gets bloated. Dr. Risley was at the farm for something else and we asked him what could be done so she could take this calf to the fair. He said she needed to find another calf. She stood with her hands on her hips, looked him in the eye and told him that was her calf, and he just needed to fix it. He came up with something so she could take it to the fair.

Later Dr. Risley would have to tell her that one of her cows had a DA and was going to die. The cow died in her arms. My kids learned life was not always fun or fair.

CHAPTER 5

We have spent many years taking a dream and turning it into a successful business. Now events unfolded that one after another turned a successful business into an unforeseen disaster that will lead to a totally new direction in life for us. I will lead you through the months and years of discovery, anguish, disappointment, disbelief, frustration, and, finally, the will to fight back, to make a difference.

December 10, 1998, having rather forgotten the Christmas party, we proceeded with everyday life. We had just finished chores; we were filling out an evaluation form that Consumers Energy had on one of their people. The man had been taking measurements to make sure the "split-neutral" was working last fall, A split-neutral is a wire sometimes called a down ground that goes down the pole from the transformer, allowing excess electricity to go into the ground. It was the first time we had seen them at the farm doing this type of work.

There was a knock at the door; Bill Hendricks from Consumers was here. He came in and said, "I hear you believe you may have a 'stray voltage' problem?" How were we supposed to know? We didn't deal with electricity and we had not even thought about it enough to have anyone check it out yet. Why was Consumers Energy sending someone to our house to ask questions? Who had told them we had any concerns? We had not seen anyone since the Christmas party.

We asked if Consumers would do testing to see if there might be a problem. No, they do not do testing. I said, "You know the one thing farmers all have in common is electricity." Mr. Hendricks got a little upset with this statement, I don't know why. He said that electricity was his business and we did not know anything about it.

Then he proceeded to say the problem on the farms was due to the farmers all using untested bulls.

"Now wait a minute. That is our business." Brian said. "All the bulls that were AI bulls are tested for a number of different things. I'm on the state board for NorthStar, a bull stud, and I know the procedures that the semen goes through before it goes on the farms."

Finally, before Mr. Hendricks left, he did agree to come back and check out the drinkers and our wiring to see if there were any farm problems. And, lo and behold, he agreed for Consumers to do a twenty-four hour test to measure voltage in the milking parlor.

Consumers have this logo: COUNT ON US. How naïve and trusting we were. All I knew about electricity is when you turn on a light switch, the lights work or if you touch a live wire, it can kill you. We believed that if a problem was found Consumers would help us correct it. After all, COUNT ON US.

About two weeks after Mr. Hendricks appeared at our door, he came back with my brother-in-law, who had done most of our farm wiring. He measured all of the drinkers on the farm and looked at the farm wiring. He declared no problems with the drinkers and that we were one of best-wired farms in the state. He would be back in a couple of weeks to do the twenty-four hour testing.

We still were having cow problems. Dr. Eyth would ask Dr. Risley to give a second opinion, and he would write a letter making several suggestions; one of which was to investigate for "stray voltage." He would also take stomach pH's to see if acidosis was a problem. Acidosis is a disorder that cows can get that puts them off feed; going off feed can make one of the cow's stomachs fill with gas and create a DA. All the pH's came back within the normal levels.

In the meantime, the other farmer, Victor Mier, who lives about eight miles from us, came and brought a couple of guys from Canada. He had purchased a system called Agrivolt, which was supposed to balance problems with the electricity coming from the utility company. They were working on his system and while they were here they could test and see if the utility was causing us problems. They tested. Yes, there were problems according to them, and they could help us for $30,000.00.

Wait a minute that is a lot of money. Are they just trying to make a sale? There are a couple of systems already in the area. Let's see if they are still doing the job in six months. We will also wait for Consumers to test and see if they back up that we have a problem.

CHAPTER 6

JANUARY–MAY 1999

One day Brian went down to our heifer barn to breed a heifer. He locks all of them into headlocks, so they cannot get away from him. As he is watching the heifers, he notices that they are stepping, lifting one foot, then putting it down and lifting the other one. It goes down the line from one to another doing the same thing.

Hey, this does not look right. It's January 28. He comes home to get the video camera to film the heifers so he can show it to Consumers when they come to test. Consumers came back a couple of weeks later, Steve Wallenwine and Bill Hendricks. I thought of them as Mutt and Jeff; Steve Wallenwine was short, with sandy, reddish hair, and Bill Hendricks was tall with a mustache.

They set up their equipment and leave it overnight. The next day when they come back to get their equipment, I ask for the test results but they can't give it to me on site. It has to be downloaded and they will bring back a report.

Brian shows them the video to look at, along with Fred Hinkley from MSU Cooperative Extension. Consumers says at first it's just flies bothering the heifers. Brian says in January there are no flies. Then Consumers says its just habit. It still does not look right.

We have always had a good working relationship with MSU. We have gone to almost all the meetings and seminars they have ever had. Therefore, we now ask Phil Durest, the Dairy Extension Agent, to look at our DHIA report. Our concern was that our freshening heifers were not producing as quickly as they should, and we ask him to see if he could find a reason.

Acidosis was again a possible concern, but we always period-ically check our nutrition rations. His report does not make a case for acidosis, but raises some other questions that we felt needed further investigation.

We will hire NorthStar, a consulting division of the company we get our bull semen from to breed our cows, to evaluate our herd and see if they could find out why production is down. Heifer peaks have been a concern. Reproduction levels were low. They will look at the overall picture.

Steve Wallenwine and Bill Hendricks from Consumers, return to deliver their report. Steve first tells me that MSU has done studies on "stray voltage" and all the voltage levels they found are within the levels. I tell him that those studies were done in the late 1980's and that the demand for electricity has grown since then and that I had learned that the voltages on the utility lines have been increased and that new studies need to be done at the new levels because no one knows what the present levels will do to cows. It will be the last time we talk about the MSU studies.

According to the report, there is voltage in the milking parlor, but Steve assures us that these levels are all within their guidelines. The same is true when we ask about voltage on the other graphs. The pages with the second-by-second counts are blank. Again, we are assured there are no problems on our farm. When we asked if we could be an electrical magnetic field from their communication tower, we were told that could not be causing any problems.

We would again have Bill Hendricks, Consumers, come out when we measured two volts on a bolt in a wooden manager down at our heifer barn using a fluke meter that Consumers gave us.

We contacted Bill Hendricks and he told us to get a Simpson meter and measure it again. We called my brother-in-law who is an electrician. He brought his Simpson meter, and again they measured voltage where there should not have been any. Consumers would again declare no problems, but would suggest we turn off the electricity to our heifer barn. The electricity would remain off until October.

We tell them we are going to look for a medical or nutritional reason for our problems, and if one cannot be found, we will return to investigate electricity. I really want to believe that there is some other reason besides electricity for the problems we are experiencing.

CHAPTER 7

We now start to investigate in earnest. Dr. Eyth cannot understand what is going on on our farm. If we have any more cows die, we will send tissue samples to MSU and see what they can come up with as a solution.

We have hired NorthStar consulting team to come and dissect our operation. They will look at our DHIA records. We take samples once a month of the milk from each cow. It is measured for butterfat, protein and somatic cell count—the bacteria found in raw milk. The tester also weighs the amount of milk each cow gives. He also records the date of birth of each calf, sex of each calf, date of breeding, and the bull used. The dates when cows are dried up to rest until the birth of her calf, dates cows die or are sold. After the new system is put into place, we will enter the information ourselves. The tester will still come once a month and weigh the milk. My Dad was on DHIA since 1955, so we have records on all the animals for forty-five years.

When NorthStar comes up, they will measure each feed: haylage, corn silage, hay, and hi-moisture corn. They take a sample from the silos and measure particle size to see if it is the right length. They then go out in the bunk feeder and take a sample and separate each feed and measures particle size there. They can not find any problem with the particle size in the feed.

NorthStar will see something they cannot understand from our records that has not been seen in all the records we have kept for the past forty-five years. Our heifers do not peak normally. When cows have a calf, they start to produce milk and that range acts like a curve. The peak is the most milk they give during their lactation—time from one calf to another.

After they peak, they produce less milk until it is time to give them a rest and they get dried up which means giving no milk until they have their next calf. Our peaks were not at a normal range. The fresh cows having had their babies seem to take longer to peak. Then they seem to catch up at the middle to the end of their lactation. The curve flat lines in the middle instead of being a normal curve.

They look at all the cows. We have too many lame cows. They comment that our cows sit like dogs, and they are concerned about cow comfort. They make some suggestions, which we try to implement. A small area in each alley in the barn needs to be grooved and the free stalls could be replaced.

We groove the floors. The free stalls in our barn have been replaced a couple of times over the years. Each time they had been installed per manufacturer measurements. It is very expensive to replace them now, and the new stalls are a lot bigger in dimension, and now MSU recommends an area in front of the cow's head so they have more room to get up.

Having built our free stall barn in the late 70's and added on in the early 80's the industry had made changes in free stall size. It will cost us a lot of money to put in new free stalls. We will have to add onto both sides of the barn to get lunge space for the cows to get up.

We replace a section of stalls on each side of the barn in the center where we take out a wall and they can lunge into the alley. We again follow manufacture instructions as to space, width, and height to place the stalls.

I count the number of cows lying in the free stalls at the same times as before and different times. No more cows lay in the new stalls than lay in the old stalls.

In fact, we have a couple of stalls next to our return alley that are shorter than all the other stalls in the barn, due to a door having to slide in front of the stalls. Cows always are laying in them each time I count cows. At this time, we cannot justify the expense to do the entire barn.

Cow comfort seems to be a concern. It might cause a cow not to milk as much, but it does not interfere with the immune system. Brian visits several other farms, that are not having any problems like ours, and he measures their free stalls. They measure the same as ours, the same width, length and height. And one has stalls a lot smaller than ours, so that each cow lays the same way in order to have enough room. They also seem to have more cows using the free stalls.

Monty Riechard, our Purina specialist, gives us his view on what we need to do. In his letter he apologizes for not recognizing in time the extent that we have been critiqued. We have been pulled apart since we opened the door for evaluation.

He told us that the dairy industry is full of persons ready and very willing and able to point out their opinions of limiting areas in your dairy operations. In time producers are to a point that they feel they might as well give up. We were assured that we were not doing things wrong and NOT to give up. He further pointed out that his pet peeve is animal exercise as Dr. Risley's is cow comfort. He thinks we might need to exercise the dry cows more. We have outside lots for all of our animals.

We let the milking herd out part of the day to exercise. Dr. Risley will say he does not see them out. He has forgotten all the times he has had to help sort cows. Or treat a cow out in the dry lot. We usually try to have the cows penned in the barn when the vet comes so we do not waste his time. We will have many opinions from everyone.

We ask because we care about our cows and a suggestion might prove to be the answer we are looking for to solve our problem. We open ourselves up to be dissected. Phil Durst from the Cooperative Extension sends Roger Mellenberger from MSU to visit us. His specialty is mastitis, not a problem we have had. We use an alley scraper which runs every two hours for an hour. I believe that this keeps the area between the free stalls clean, as well as the place where the cows lay to rest or sleep and the bunk, the area where the cows eat, so we do not have a high somatic cell count. Although I would like to see the somatic cell count lower.

Dr. Mellenberger suggests that we take more of the wall off our holding pen which we will do. Also, we could use a bigger water fountain at the end of the barn by the holding pen, and so we install a larger water fountain. He also suggests we take the roof vent back several more inches. No one goes up to measure how wide the opening is now. If we get too much air in the barn in the winter our alley scraper will freeze up. It's one suggestion we cannot do.

The barn was built in 1978, and we constructed for the recommendations at that time. Today barns are built with higher roofs, but the barns built before ours were tightly enclosed with fans to remove the warm air from the animals. As the years go by changes are made; new ideas are tried. One idea does not make another idea wrong. For example, some people still use stanchion barns instead of milking parlors and this method does not kill cows. We have a major problem. Because we are good managers, no one can understand what is happening. We should not be losing cows all of a sudden after managing our farm for thirty-one years and having over 100 years of experience between us, did we wake up one morning stupid?

Did we forget all of the classes we had taken on nutrition—an eight-week course, or on fertility, another eight-week course, or all the other courses the MSU put on in our area that we attended? I do not think so; we have to find out what is causing our cows to die.

On February 25, 1999, two cows die. The veterinarian takes tissue samples to send to MSU. The results come back. These cows have Lymphosarcoma, and are positive for Bovine Leucosis or leukemia. I call our vet; I am so relieved we have finally found out what is wrong with our cows.

I ask him what we can use to vaccinate the cows. He says there is no vaccine for Bovine Leucosis and not to worry. It is not a big problem in herds. One cow out of 100 dies every three years and they are old cows. Okay; we will not worry about it; problem solved.

March 31, 1999, Animal 1453's diagnosis—lymphosarcoma; the next month, Animal 1398 went down—necropsy, found perforated ulcer, did not test for lymphosarcoma. In May, 1999, Animal 1572 tests positive for lymphosarcoma. She went down and could not get up. She had to be destroyed. MSU calls concerned about how old the cow is; are we sure she is only four years old? They have not seen lymphosarcoma in animals this young.

Things are starting to get scary. I start to look for information on Bovine leucosis. Bovine Leucosis, adult form, occurs in dairy cattle older than two years of age with peak incidence in five-eight year old cattle. National Animal Health Monitoring System Dairy 1996 study showed widespread distribution of bovine leucosis virus (BLV).Herd prevalence in the Midwest was 89% with approximately 40% of animals being infected.

The numbers were similar around the country, although the southeast had higher herd and animal prevalence rates.

The numbers are higher than those in Canada where a survey found forty percent of herds are infected. The European Economic Community nations, which have a strict control program, rarely exceed 0.5 to 1.5% per prevalence. The report also says that Lymph nodes located near the surface can be detected by touch. They are also visible on the cows' necks.

I contact Dr. David J. Sprecher who has written articles on this. He tells me the same thing as our veterinarians. There are only a couple of herds where it has really been a problem. One of them is in Virginia; the other is Carnation Farms in Oregon. Dr. Sprecher advises me to use a needle per cow when giving shots, to single sleeve each cow we check for pregnancy, and to identify positive cows and non-positive cows. Only feed milk to the calves from non-positive cows. Watch fly control, as flies can also spread it. Bovine Leucosis is not dangerous to humans.

Okay, I now talk to Dr. Monkey; he oversees the bulls at Select Sires, a bull stud farm, in Ohio. He tells me the same thing; BL should not be a problem; it does not kill cows. I call Dr. Chris Ashworth, a Purina Veterinarian, who has written an article on Bovine Leukemia Virus—Bovine Leucosis. He tells me the same story, but his report says to disinfect all equipment used to dehorn as well as anything dealing with blood. His report also says Lymphosarcoma is the most common cancer of cattle. I finally call Carnation Farms in Oregon since they have had a large problem and overcame the issue, and they tell me the same things to do.

We now have to decide how many of our animals have BLV. Dr. Eyth says we need to take a random group, test them, and see how prevalent it is in our herd. Purina will test twenty animals for us free of charge.

I open the holding pen and tell the guy to watch the gate and let me know when we have twenty animals. When the test results are in, we could not have hand picked a better selection. Out of the twenty animals, ten animals were born before 1995 and ten animals were born after 1995. We now have our split.

Of the ten cows born before 1995, three were positive for BLV. Of the ten animals born after 1995, seven were positive. This would later prove to be very significant. We now knew that of the twenty animals 50 % were positive for Bovine leukemia.

We immediately implemented a control program. Any veterinarian on our farm used a single needle to Bangs vaccinate, as would we on any shot we gave. All equipment used for dehorning was sanitized with each use, and individual sleeves were used for any examination of any animal. We used only milk from non-positive cows to feed our calves. We're good at looking for symptoms for cows with BLV. We would sell another cow that had tested positive, was acting weak, and was going down on milk.

CHAPTER 8

JULY–AUGUST 1999

July 6, 1999, Animal 1468 came down with two bloody quarters. She was tested and found positive. After three weeks of not clearing up she was sold. We also have called in Dr. Rhoda Clark for a second opinion. She sends in tests on 1468, which shows the cow's immune system has been affected.

During the next week, Animal 1458 freshened, came down with acute mastitis and died. Animal 1472 freshened and died of kidney failure. Animal 1465 freshened and came down with a leg infection and died about a week later. Animal 1430 went down and died. Necropsy showed lesions. Animal 1174 died of heart failure. At this time, we started to visibly pick up lesions on necks or ribs of a number of cows. As you can imagine by this time, I am a basket case. The cows are my responsibility. I have the vet out. Nothing is working! My cows will not stop dying! I cry all the time!

The feed salesmen come; I cry. The bull semen salesmen come; I cry. The DHIA tester comes; I cry. The things that use to work do not any more. It's so frustrating. We have spent all of our lives around cows. We have had several times that we ran into trouble with the cows; once we ran into fat cow syndrome which is when cows eat too much and get too fat. They have trouble when they have their calves. But all we had to do was separate the cows into groups and feed them according to whether they were milking or dry, waiting to have a calf. This time nothing seems to work. Having all the people come and do testing on feed, or changing free stalls, or any other suggestion are not stopping the cows from dying. We have always tried to keep up with new technology so our equipment is not antiquated.

We had invested in a Heat Watch system a couple of years ago. Heat Watch uses a transponder that is glued on the animal's back just in front of the tail. When that animal is in heat, another animal will ride her and set off the transponder. The signal is sent to a receiver in the barn that transfers the information to a computer. The system worked well for several years. In 1999 it quit. Cows were not riding each other to trigger the transponder.

We used the outside lots for both cows and the heifers so they would have better footing. Nothing seemed to work. The heifers had always been easier to get pregnant. We use to joke that it was not any use checking them as Brian had an excellent rate. We had always had them in an outside lot until we built our heifer barn in 1992. Then they were confined inside of the barn, and we could not see them. We had a little trouble getting them bred until we made an outside lot. We could see it from our house; we watched it at every meal, and the kids were sent out a lot to get the number of the animal. They got very good at watching for heats. We all watched. It was your job any time any one was around the animals.

Because we could not identify heats any more, we went to using a new method of giving shots to the animals to artificially bring them into heat. We used a product called Cysterlene. That worked a little better, but it was expensive. Our veterinarian recommended a cheaper product. We discovered that it did not have as much concentration of the ingredient, and though it worked well on other farms in the area, it would not work for us. We had to go back to Cysterlene. We were the only farm to have to use it for better results, so it had to be ordered special for us. We started to talk about normal farms and our farm.

When we had to sedate a cow to take care of a DA, twisted stomach, we had to give them more medicine than they used on other farms. In addition, we had to give a higher dose of antibiotics than other farms. Even the Cysterlene did not work as well as some thought it should and everyone who came on the farm recommended we use a bull.

Bulls are dangerous; using a bull to breed our cows was the recommendation I did not take to that idea very well. Brian subjected himself to having someone watch to see if he did things right when he bred the animals. He had only been doing it since 1970 without any problems. Must be he forgot all he had learned after all these year!

Everyone looks at us with pity and no answers. I can not help my cows. I am at the end of the rope. I have had about all I can take.

Over the years, we have had a successful business. Now all of a sudden, it is falling apart, and we do not seem to be able to stop it.

We had grown up knowing farming as a way of life. At some point in the last few years, someone had decided it had to be treated as a business. So Cooperative Extension MSU had held a seminar and we had written a Mission Statement:

"Our mission is to produce a superior quality dairy product through the wise use of our resources. We strive to achieve a standard of living for the family and employees that allows us to enjoy a balance of work and leisure time, while maintaining efficiency. We take pride in being leaders in the use of new technology as it and monetary resources become available, in owning land and well-kept machinery, in producing quality feed, the result being the production of quality of milk that makes us an asset to our community and the dairy industry. We humbly accept the responsibilities, which God has given us to carry out."

Our mission statement states every thing we believed in concerning the responsibility we felt toward our animals, and now we could do nothing to help them. After all these years, we were letting our animals down that had been placed in our care. They are totally dependent on us; they can not talk and tell us what is wrong with them. Oh, how I wish they could.

No one wanted to believe us, and no one will want to believe what we will find. After the five cows died, I have come to the end of the road; no one can understand how I feel. How totally responsible I feel. We have put heart and soul into this farm. What disappointment I feel. I prayed, "God help me, I can't do this alone. I will write a book telling our story." Little did I know God would answer my prayers in such an earth shattering way or what kind of a road He would send us down!

Chapter 9

July 30, 1999

Something had triggered the immune system to quit functioning on our herd. Dr. Eyth called MSU veterinarian Dr. Ron Erskine and asked his team to come up. We met with them all; our vet, Extension, Purina. That day about fifteen people came to our farm—the hottest day of the year. After spending all day looking at everything, taking stomach pH samples which were all in the normal range, they concluded the only disease that could cause this kind of devastation was BVD, Bovine Viral Diarrhea. Dr. Erskine would arrange for Dr. Grooms and Dr. Pilar to come and take blood samples from all the adult animals and test for BVD and Bovine leukemia.

As the group was getting ready to leave, Victor Mier and a representative from the Attorney General's office, Marty May, pulled in the driveway. It seemed a little strange that the group from MSU left immediately instead of watching Vic and Marty do electrical measurements.

It was the first time we had met Marty May. He took measurements of the voltage going down Consumer's down ground which is only thirty feet from the front of our barn. There were fourteen and one half volts going down the down ground. We would later learn what that would mean. Consumers maxed out on electrical usage for 1999 that day (used the most electricity at any one time).

Victor told us that David Stetzer, an electrician from Wisconsin, was at his farm and had been testing all day for voltage. He invited us to come over and meet Mr. Stetzer.

Mr. Stetzer had a trailer with a lot of equipment and had gadgets every where. We were curious as to what he was measuring and how the equipment worked. Was this for real? Could there really be some problem with the electricity each of us had running to our farms. Electricity is a factor we all have in common.

We were telling Mr. Stetzer that Bovine Leukemia had been found in our cows. He did not say a word. Just went into his trailer and brought out a book. The book is titled "The Zapping of America—Microwaves, Their Deadly Risk, and the Cover-up" by Paul Brodeur. He opened it to Chapter four, page forty-three. The part he had highlighted said, "The mice were irradiated at a power density of 100 mill watts per square centimeter for four and a half minutes a day, over a period of fifty-nine weeks. The longevity of the mice did not appear to be affected by these conditions. However, when the researchers performed autopsies on irradiated animals that had died during the course of the experiment, and compared them with autopsies performed on control animals that had not been exposed to microwaves, they discovered testicular degeneration in forty percent of the dead irradiated mice, and in only eight percent of the control.

Even more alarming, they found cancer of the white blood cells—both lymphatic leucosis and lymphatic leukemia in fully thirty-five percent of the irradiated mice, as compared with ten percent of the controls."

I cried!!! The communication tower one quarter mile from our farm runs on microwaves. Stetzer told us we needed to ask Consumers to come back and test for harmonics and transients.

Electricity supplied by utilities such as Consumers is of the alternating current, "AC", variety. This means that it cycles sixty times per second. A "harmonic" is an electrical signal that alternates at some higher frequency that is a multiple of the sixty times per second. A "third harmonic," for example, alternates at a rate of 180 cycles per second. Transients are temporary, unwanted voltage in a circuit. The most frequent cause of oscillatory transients are the sudden release of stored energy due to unfiltered electrical equipment, contact bounce, arcing, and electricity being switched on and off. Increased use of solid state electronic equipment such as computers, printers, variable speed drives, and power-line switching to balance loads contribute to increased numbers of transients.

We call Bill Hendricks, a farm representative for Consumers, the next day. We ask him to test for transients and harmonics. His reply is "Where did you hear the word harmonics?" I said to Brian, "We just found the right buzz word."

A few days go by and we receive a letter from Steve Wallenwine. He also was on our farm earlier and did testing for Consumers. He requested any measurements that had been taken on our farm. The only testing that had been done by anyone outside of Consumers was Marty May from the Attorney General's office. We did not have a copy of the results. Bill Hendricks would make an appointment to come out and again do "stray voltage" measurements in our barn.

Eventually they would reschedule. They had planned to come the same week as the Ogemaw County Fair. The whole area complains about a loss of power during fair time. The fair requires so much electricity that transformers have burned up. If voltage is low that week, no wonder Consumers does not want to take any measurements.

I talk to our son, Kevin, and I tell him about the "harmonics". He is in his third year at Michigan State University studying to be a mechanical engineer. He says to me, "Mom, we studied "harmonics" in class. They are harmful, nasty business. You need to contact my professor at MSU." I phone his professor, who will remain anonymous

. He says yes there is a problem and it needs to be investigated immediately. I ask him to recommend someone who knows what to test for and how to do the test. He warns me to stay away from Ag. Engineering at MSU, they are not unbiased, but he recommends a retired professor whom he thinks would be honest.

We, as well as Cooperative Extension agent Fred Hinkley, contact Professor Parks, but Parks is building a house in Montana and will be gone for a while. Another dead end.

We also test twenty animals for BVD (Bovine viral diarrhea) seven to twelve months of age who have never been vaccinated. We were having trouble with several cows and ten heifers fourteen to twenty months of age. So now we have tested animals in each of our three barns. If we have a problem with BVD, it should show up in these groups. All the tests were negative for BVD but found another ten had Bovine leukemia.

Finally Steve Wallenwine and Bill Hendricks come out to test for "stray voltage". They put a copper plate on the floor of the milking parlor to measure voltage in the milking parlor. Then we bring the cows in to milk, when the meter reads .023 volts, the cows kick the milkers off. I try to get Steve and Bill to come and watch, but they won't come into the parlor to watch. They tell me that the measurements are within the levels. We also ask them to go down and measure the barn where the electricity has been turned off since March. They refuse. I ask them to bring an oscilloscope to measure ground current.

We look at a group of cows I put in so they can see how bad they look. Number 1370 is one of those cows. She is one that won the Junior two-year-old award from DHIA in 1996. She is now so thin she looks like she is going to die. How I wish cows could talk.

Steve tries to be sympathetic. He says he can understand what we are going through. His wife's folk's farm lost a barn in a fire. He wishes he could help, but it is not electricity causing our problems. He wishes us good luck on finding the problem through MSU.

We again ask about the communication tower. He tells us it is an 880 MHz tower, the most powerful, so as not to have low level problems.

I also have read in Brodeur's book that microwaves can cause decreased memory. I have been having problems remembering things this summer and I have also had my thyroid medicine reduced for the first time in sixteen years. When exposed to microwaves the thyroid over produces and the studies also identify a short term memory loss. I tell this to Steve and Bill of Consumers. We ask them to come back and conduct measurements Electro-Magnetic Fields, EMF, and ground measurements with an oscilloscope which measures electric current in the earth. They decide to come back. They appear to be trying to be helpful except they wouldn't watch the cows kick off the milkers, etc.

In the next couple of weeks there is a lot of activity at the substation. Trucks spent all day there for several days in a row. In our experience we had hardly ever seen any activity at the substation. Even others in the neighborhood had noticed the number of people at the substation and had commented on it.

After whatever work done at the substation was completed, we notice the first activity of cows riding each other, signs of being in heat. For several days in a row we are again getting heat activity that has not been there for many months.

Steve Wallenwine and Bill Hendricks came back on August 23 and leave me a stack of material about "stray voltage". One article was the Minnesota Study, which Steve points out to me. One of the study's conclusions was that 1 milliamp of the 60 hertz electrical current for two weeks had no significant effect on the immune function of dairy cattle. It is the only article he comments about. I ask him, "How you can know the long term effect on cows in only two weeks?"

I finally get a chance a couple of days later to read more articles.

Another article defines "stray voltage" as a small voltage less than ten volts measured between two points that can be contacted simultaneously by an animal.

The Minnesota Study that Steve pointed out to us to show us that we did not have a problem was a mail and telephone survey sent out to 2500 dairy farmers in Minnesota and Wisconsin. 752 (30%) farmers completed the survey.

The article concluded that problems on these farms were due to poor nutrition, poor cow comfort and hygiene, and low or no use of vaccinations and related preventive veterinary practices, and those who want to improve performance of dairy herds should always address these factors. I'm beginning to learn that the utility companies seem to always blame the farmer.

CHAPTER 10

SEPTEMBER 1999

We are still experiencing too many sick cows. It takes an extra hour each day to take temperatures, pen fresh cows and give them extra hay to prevent DA, twisted stomach. I now have to make a list to keep track of which cow I'm treating because there are so many. We have to have the vet out at least once a week.

MSU came and took samples of all the adult animals to see if they have BVD. I begged Dr. Dan Grooms to find us a disease. We could vaccinate for that and work our way out of the problem in a couple of years; otherwise he will be sending us down a road that I do not want to travel. The tests all come back negative; there are no diseases on our farm except BLV (Bovine Leucosis).

At this point we are pretty frustrated. Dr. Eyth writes us a letter.

To whom it may concern:

There has been a perceptible decline in health and production of the Bellville herd over the last several years.

There has been a dramatic increase in cow mortality to such a degree that Bellville's can no longer produce enough replacement heifers to maintain the size of their herd. We do know that the herd has an infection rate of approximately 50% with Bovine Leucosis. A large number of animals have died due to this disease in the last six months (approximately).

Bovine Leucosis is a common disease but usually accompanied by a low rate of transmission and a very low death rate. We feel that both the rate of transmission and death rates are due to presently unknown factors which have caused immunosuppression, meaning decreased resistance to infection. So far infectious disease factors, such as BVD and Johne's, have all come back negative. We are attempting to determine any factors which would add stress to this herd, but so far have been unable to identify any.

Historically, Bellville's have been good dairy producers, exhibiting excellent management skills, with good cow health and accompanying production. Mortality figures were never high and health problems were similar to other well-managed herds.

Sincerely,

Timothy H. Eyth, D.V.M.

We greatly appreciated our veterinarian's letter. At least he believes there is a problem on our farm, even if he does not know what the problem could be.

David Camp, our State representative in Washington, paid us a visit when we contacted his office. He looked at our facilities and we showed him the video of the heifers stepping in January. He feels there is some kind of problem; we have a good-looking farm and should not be experiencing problems. He might be able to talk to Consumers and get them to help us. He might have more influence with Consumers and maybe they will start to change the electricity on our farm.

Without finding a medical problem, we continue to look at the electrical aspect. In the literature Consumers brought, there is any article on sheep. It says a study found no effect of EMF (Electro Magnetic Fields) on sheep raised beneath a transmission line in Oregon. There were no effects on the reproductive cycles: however, a possible effect on the immune system was found.

In another article, a study done in Iowa on sheep infected with Bovine leukemia virus had been exposed to electric and magnetic fields. Are we in a field from the communication tower?

I contact Iowa University where the study was done. Dr. Lyle Miller, who did the research, had retired and moved to Illinois, but they give me his telephone number. I call Dr. Miller; he is surprised that I tracked him down. He tells me that no one took measurements of the current in the ground, only the overhead current from the transmission lines. He also knows about the other study that made the connection with the immune system. He sends me an article on the effects of continuous low-intensity irradiation on the immune system. It reveals a wide variety of immune modifying effects. Immune system homeostasis disturbances develop with the time of irradiation to form a secondary immune deficiency. He gives me a telephone number in Maryland that may be able to direct me to others doing immunologic studies relating to EMF.

Maryland directs me to Oregon where I talk to the Professor who oversaw the sheep study that had the immune response. Yes, he confirmed, they had an immune suppression from the EMF field. He also said there had been studies done in Canada on cows. In the literature from Consumers I found the article.

I called McGill University in Montreal and located Dr. J. Burchard. He confirmed that the study found that in addition to any effects on neurotransmitter systems, EMF may alter permeability of the blood-brain barrier. If this blood-brain barrier is broken, it causes major health issues. A number of our cows have had neurological problems; they go down and never get back up.

A blood sample can measure Quinolinic acid levels. Quinolinic acid levels would show a significant 2.4 fold increase during exposure to the EMF field, which would not return to baseline after exposure. I talk to Dr. Eyth, but he has not heard of this, and it takes a special laboratory to do the tests. I ask Dr. Eyth if we could do these tests to see if the Quinolinic acid levels would prove we were an EMF field. MSU does not have the capabilities at the animal laboratory to run these tests. Another wall that no one wants to climb.

In the meantime, I have talked to a Dr. Andy Johnson from Wisconsin. Wisconsin has a large number of farms with electrical problems. I ask him if he would visit our farm, telling him what we have tested for and done. He says that what we have done is what he would suggest, so there is no point in him making the trip.

We have also located a farmer north by Alpena who is having the same problems we are experiencing. He has had a lot of abortions. We have lost calves in about eight heifers that had been confirmed pregnant. Brian and Victor Mier go to talk to him. Alpena Power spent three days on his farm. They moved his Primary Neutral, the electrical wire, from his transformer that lets the unused electricity go into the ground to the other side of the road. The farmer's veterinarian said "It was like night and day. It made a huge difference." We ask Dr. Eyth to contact her. Maybe we can get Consumers to move our Primary Neutral to the other side of the road away from the barn, a really simple solution. Consumers Energy has notified us that they will be here on Friday of Labor Day weekend to do EMF measurements. I contact Stetzer the electrician from Wisconsin. He said in July that if we could get Consumers to come back and test, he would test at the same time. He is unable to come. I also contact the Attorney General's office and ask if someone could come and observe the testing.

During the next few days I called my daughter, Dawn in Kalamazoo. She says, "Mom, why is a different number than yours showing up on my caller ID?" I have no idea. Dawn and her husband milk cows in Kalamazoo. Lori has moved to work in Washington D.C. Andrea is working in Connecticut with Pepperidge Farms as an ingredient purchaser. Kevin is still at Michigan State University and Kay is still at home. They have all been very good supporting us. As they know the problems we are experiencing were never present when they were home growing up and working on the farm.

Chapter 11

September–November 1999

My daughter, Lori and her boyfriend decide to come home over Labor Day weekend from Washington D.C. Friday of Labor Day weekend finally arrives. Now maybe we can get to the bottom of our problem. Consumers arrive with five people. We have a number of people here to watch them conduct their tests.

But once again all they bring is hand held equipment, not an oscilloscope. They explain that there is an electrical and a magnetic field and they test for each in every building. Marty May from the AG's office has us ask them to switch from measuring 60 Hz to 180 Hz which shows harmonics. Harmonics is the distortion of the 60 Hz cycle, as we learn. Yes, it shows we have harmonics, but Consumers won't keep on that level. They keep switching it back to 60 Hz.

They are also going to show us that the tower can't be causing a problem. One guy talks on a walkie talkie, and it makes the other guy's walkie talkie beep. What a joke. Walkie talkies are not the same communication as the truck's radios. How do we know that this test means anything? Of course, they are taking all the measurements after 2:00 p.m. on Friday afternoon on Labor Day weekend. How many of their trucks are communicating with each other that day?

After finding out my daughter's boyfriend is from Washington D.C., one of the men from Consumers' keeps sidling up to him and asking him where he works. Maybe Consumers thinks we have the government investigating them. Steve Wallenwine finally gets around to telling us there is nothing wrong on our farm.

He gets to the Bovine Leukemia. He thinks we brought it in with the other animals that were here for a year and we spread it by using a common needle. Because that is the only disease we have, Consumers has to blame it on something.

I have been waiting all day for him to bring up the Bovine Leukemia. I said, "Remember the first twenty animals we tested back in July. Three of the positive animals were born before 1995 and seven of those animals were born after 1995. In looking at the records on these animals, the communication tower started operation in September of 1994. The three cows that were born before 1995 were still in the heifer barn which is in a direct line with the communication tower; the animal's positive with BLV except one came out of that barn and are dated to when the tower became active."

Once again I request that they bring an oscilloscope. Steve says they only take that piece of equipment to office building that have a lot of computers. I ask him if those buildings are more important than my cows. He looks at me and says he will find out if they can bring it to our farm and run some more tests.

Our daughter, Lori, spends the weekend putting our DHIA records on a graph. She says "Mom, what happened in 1996? Your herd average went up each year until then and that year it dropped." She also plotted health records, sick cows, dead cows, reasons cows left the herd.

We could not find any health reasons for the drop in milk. But when I thought about it, I said in January of 1996 our grocery store opened up again after being closed for several years. They had trouble with their compressors and replaced them in October of that year. From January to October is when we got the drop in milk, and then it went back up.

Diane's herd was here that year and I could not make sense of why her cows gave an average of 60# of milk per month and ours gave an average of 40#. I still do not understand what is going on. This is the first time we have ever put a number of years' records together to compare them.

After Labor Day I contact Dave Stetzer the electrician from Wisconsin. The first thing he said to me was that my phone's tapped. He was an intelligence officer in Vietnam. I say, "Right." But while I am talking to him I hear a click on the phone. Brian goes to an Iosco Intermediate School board meeting and tells someone about this conversation. The board member tells him that if your phone is tapped you hear a click.

I call Dawn and she wants to know why the telephone number is listing a different number than ours. This goes on for a couple of weeks. The click starts at 10:00 a.m. and continues until 5:00 p.m. Other people we talk to can hear it also. There will be a total of nine numbers show up. My son-in law does not believe it until one day when I called them. Somehow the phone does not disconnect and he heard two guys talking about wireless phones. We had just been saying they had not found our cell phones yet. Finally, I call the phone company. Yes, the other number I give them is a working number. When I call this number, no one answers. They are within a block of numbers usually given to businesses, but they won't give me any names. I ask if we can have a check done to see if our phone is tapped.

The day the repairman comes he is here for several hours. While he is checking it out; the numbers change like they are being rotated. Because our long distance crosses into another company's area, he can't find anything. The clicking will continue from September through the middle of January. A year later the AG's office would investigate after one of their attorney's house was broken into and some of his mail was removed. He was in charge of their case against Consumers. It is against the law to have your phone tapped unless court ordered. For us this felt like an invasion of our privacy, but we did not say anything; we did not want Consumers to know. Trying to prove it was happening proved to be impossible. But after hearing some of the things that had been done to other families fighting Consumers, I did not doubt it was possible for them to be listening in our conversations hoping to gain information. About a week later, Steve Wallenwine called to say they were still working on coming again to test. He then asked about the farmer on Alpena Power to see what they had done to help him. We have hope that Consumers will move our Primary Neutral farther away from our barn. But on September 23, we receive a letter from James Schrandt, Consumers head of the Agriculture Division. His letter informs us they will not be out to do any further tests. The levels of harmonics found on our farm are not a concern. They are not going to test any ground current.

We had been searching since the end of July to find an independent firm to do testing, but most of the companies we contacted sell a device to fix the so called "stray voltage" problem like the Agrivolt system. We finally find a firm who will test and not try to sell us something. On September 25, we start to test for a week. During this time there was a lot of activity at the substation one day.

Cooperative Extension had found a veterinarian from Ohio, who had worked on farms with electrical problems. They set up a meeting with him to come and look at our farm. He wanted to look at our DHIA and herd health records.

After he had access to this information, we learned he had been paid $1,628,400.00 by Consumers Energy. Imagine our shock; I thought we were getting an unbiased opinion. I had been warned not to let him take pictures. In one case he testified for the utility that a farmer had rats as big as dogs on his farm, so that made the farmer a poor manager. In another case, the farmer ground feed for his neighbor's pigs, Dr. Sanders took a feed sample and said the farmer fed the feed to his cows and that was the cause of his problems. In spite of what we knew, we decide to meet and hear what he had to say

When Dr. Sanders got to our farm, indeed he did start to take pictures. I told him he could not, and he told us he used them to make his notes. I told him I had heard of his pictures and he'd have to rely on his memory today. We spent several hours in our office. He did not take any measurements of any kind.

He looked at our cows from the outside of the barn, did not walk through them or get close to them. He did not watch any of the milking. He did tell me he had contacted Consumers to tell them he was coming up to our farm.

At this point I told him, he must have been good at deducing "stray voltage" because Consumers puts the people who beat them on their payroll, and he had been paid $1,600,000.00, so he must have been good. He immediately wanted to know how we found that out. I would not tell him, and he spent the rest of his time at the farm trying to get that information.

Later that evening after a meeting he put on for extension, he still wanted to know how we received our information. Brian told him, he must not have done a very good job the first year because he had only been paid $50.00. He seemed to be more concerned on how we had obtained that information than anything else on his visit.

Dr. Sanders would inform Consumers that we were doing electrical testing on the farm while he was there. He tried to get information from the company doing the testing and Consumers also tried to get the report before us.

One of Dr. Sander's recommendations was that we work with a team from MSU. So a meeting was set up with MSU's Dr. Erskine, who had been here in July, MSU's nutritionist Dr. Herb Bucholtz, Purina's nutritionist Dr. Kevin Dill. Purina Sales people Scott Simpkins and Ken Helmrich, Moorman salesman Scott Closclausre were there as well as Phil Durst from the Extension office, and Dr. Ron Risley, who was sitting in for Dr. Eyth.

We went over the medical results, feed rations, etc. Results: Dr. Bucholtz will approve rations formulated by Scott Simpkins and Dr. Dill. We will keep records on feed moisture levels, feed intake, dry matter intake, milk weights, and health records. We will meet again in March to evaluate the progress we are making.

Fred Hinkley from the Cooperative Extension has found a book written by Consumers James Schrandt and MSU. In it was a list of symptoms to look for in "stray voltage" cases:

Animals that avoid a watering device or feeder

Unusual drinking or eating behavior at a waterier or feeder

When confined, animals that do not stand still but shift their weight frequently

Animals that show signs of being uncomfortable and difficult to handle

Animals that may be reluctant to enter a building or area

Animals that may run or jump out of a building or area quickly when released

Weight gain less than expected or an unexplained loss of weight

An increase incidence in clinical mastitis in dairy cows

A decrease in milk production of dairy cows not explained by seasonal or lactation change

We have noticed that our cows lap water from the drinkers; they don't want to come into the milking parlor to be milked. They have been experiencing weight loss that we did not use to have. We are not getting the milk we should. The heifers were shifting their feet. Brian took the video of that in January Consumers helped write the book. How can they deny what is going on at our farm?

The electrical report is back. It shows that our Prescott substation is not grounded. With no grounding at the substation, the electricity may have a hard time going back like it is supposed to do. It also shows we get very high voltage in our milking parlor, and even when electricity is turned off on our farm, we still have voltage. It also shows the presence of harmonics and transients at levels that should not be there.

Steve looks at the report and does not like what he sees. He questions whether the equipment was set up correctly. So I tell him to forget this report, come set up his equipment side by side with the company who did the report. We will have MSU come verify they each are set up correctly and we'll run tests for a week and let the chips fall where they may. He says they could not do that. What are they afraid of finding?

We are starting to have trouble with the cows in the milking parlor. Several go down on their front knees after the milkers are put on them. It seems to happen about the same time each day. We had a group of cows come in and the front cow went nuts pushing on the front gate. She finally fell down.

I find a dead cow when I go to milk one morning. Another cow goes down in the holding pen and never gets up again.

Another cow went down in the milking parlor and we had to pull her out. Thanksgiving Day was the worst day for both milkings. Everyone cooks turkey all day long. The cows are jumpier than normal and kick the milkers off constantly. The cows also step around more. Manure is everywhere which makes for a really dirty milking. It is frustrating, not being able to put milking units on the cows and be able to go to the next cow. Instead, I have to keep going back and put the units back on the same cows after they have kicked them off.

The day after Thanksgiving, Vic Mier calls and wants to know if my milking was better. The Primary Neutral has been disconnected, so the electricity no longer goes into the ground at our barn. By night milking, I can see a difference. It took about twelve hours and the cows quit lapping at the water. They started to come into the parlor on their own instead of us having to chase each group in to milk. We start to get more milk. They quit kicking the milkers off. They did manure in the parlor. What a difference!

But after three days, the heifers were not eating as much. Feed dropped from 1800# to 800#. The pole at that barn measures 9 volts; it is the next transformer where the voltage goes into the ground. That down ground was disconnected too, or the animals would have starved to death. This lasted for ten days until Consumers were notified that our down grounds were disconnected.

Bill Hendricks of Consumers showed up and said to me, "We received a call from Mr. Mier telling us that your Primary Neutrals are disconnected. Victor is a friend of yours, isn't he?" Needless to say, I was upset.

My cows were just getting relief. I cried and asked him how many more of our cows had to die before they would do something about the problem.

It took just twelve hours after the primary neutral was reconnected for the cows to go back to not drinking, not coming into the parlor, etc. I would also find out that Bill Hendricks had lied to me. It was Tom Muir who had called them not Victor Mier. Mr. Hendricks would later tell me I had misunderstood him.

We have investigated management, nutrition, disease and ruled out all of these, but we have electrical tests that show a problem that the utility needs to correct. Now I know that it is electricity, without a doubt. Up to this point I did not know what or who to believe. I did not want to believe Consumers would deliberately mislead us. Their logo says Count On Us. Right! Consumers would not help us.

CHAPTER 12

DECEMBER 1999

D r. Sanders has written a recommendation after his visit. He felt that there were no electrical problems on our farm. At no time did he take any electrical measurements, so I am not sure on what basis he is making that assumption. He did know that we were having the electrical study done and called the people doing the study to get information from them.

One of the graphs from the study showed that when the farm electricity was disconnected the graph should have gone to zero, but instead measured voltage still present. This is curious because where is this electricity coming from if we are disconnected from the power source?

Another graph shows that there is extremely high voltage in our milking parlor. Dr. Sanders indicates this is impossible. The study also shows high levels of harmonics. It also reveals that our substation is not grounded as it should be. Our substation may be the only one in the state having the neutral nut not connected to the earth. The neutral nut is supposed to be connected to the earth for grounding. Consumers will not tell us the location of another substation like ours in the state. For us this study raises some disturbing questions. Who is telling us the truth?

Consumers Energy's Steve Wallenwine calls and wants to see the study. We make a date for him to review it. The day he comes, he brings back some of the equipment to test for EMF, electro magnetic fields. They have had the machine calibrated which had not been done the last time they were here in September.

We learn that where we had placed our calf hutches, little huts that the calves live in for so many years and were under the distribution lines in front of our barn, measure ninety volts. We are told that the threshold is 100. This would be dangerous to their health.

Is this why so many of them died that one year?

We had a problem the day after Thanksgiving in 1989. We lost forty calves in a row. Andrea, our third daughter, would feed one in the morning and by noon it might be dead. She did not want to feed them any more. We took some to MSU and they could not find a reason for them dying. Then the calves stopped dying just as fast as they started just before Christmas when the ground froze. It looks now like there was just too much electricity going to them; it had been a wet fall. The ground is a good conductor when wet. Now where we have moved the hutches only measures five volts. We have very few calf deaths. How were we to know the location for the calf hutches could be such a problem?

Steve then wanted to look at the study done on the electricity. He started to go through the book. When he got to the graph that showed the high voltage or spike and the graph where the farm had been disconnected and still showed voltage, he said he did not know if the equipment had been hooked up properly or if it had been calibrated. I said to him, "Okay let's just close this book. You bring you're equipment and set it up and I will have the company who had done the study bring their equipment. We will set them up side by side, have MSU verify that they are connected correctly and run a test for a week. Then we will let the chips fall where they may and see who is right."

Consumers was not going to accept any thing from someone else, and, at this point, I was beginning to believe Consumers could not be trusted. Since Consumers would not accept the study, we contacted our State representative Dale Sheltrown and Michigan Farm Bureau to see if they could look at the study and make Consumers do something so that our cows could be relieved from their stress. We were becoming aware that this problem had and was occurring on farms across the state of Michigan and as well as other states.

About this time Cooperative Extension found a book, written by MSU's Truman Surbrook and Consumers Power's James Schrandt. It outlined how electricity has to make a circuit from the substation to our house or farm, and the unused electricity then travels back to the substation on the neutral wire to make the circuit. The study showed that the utility companies have been allowed to make down grounds, four per mile, for a safety factor for lightning strikes. But if the lines are not large enough, the unused electricity that has to go back to the substation is siphoned off into the earth and allowed to find its own way back using the path of least resistance which may be through my barn or your house.

We learned all we could about this electricity that went into the earth and what happens to it once it is placed there. Depending on the resistance of the earth, the ground water level and a number of other factors in the right combination, this stray electricity can cause major problems on farms.

After we contacted Farm Bureau, they had several conversations with Consumers. I receive a call from a Farm Bureau representative. He too has asked Consumers to agree to a third party electrical testing on our farm; he tells them it is not good public relations for them not to agree. If there are NO problems on our farm as the study indicates, what do they have to lose? Prove the study wrong!

It seems to me that Consumers are afraid to let someone else do testing on our farm. At this time we are still having health problems with the cows. Even though we have MSU managing the herd, we have four cows sick one night and have to call the vet out again. It has become very frustrating to have to fight this battle alone, while everyone stands on the sidelines watching our cows die.

After several weeks, Farm Bureau calls and says that they have been able to get James Schrandt (in charge of the agriculture division at Consumers) to agree to meet with us. Now we are making progress. Mr. Schrandt helped write the book that lists all the symptoms that we are experiencing. Finally, maybe he can help us!

Mr. Schrandt and Bill Hendricks come to our house on Dec. 20. We have our friend, Chuck Preston, a retired Agriculture teacher, with us. As we sit at our dining room table, we discuss what has been going on at our farm. The conversation goes as follows: Mr. Schrandt says "Is it is not electricity causing our problems."

"Mr. Schrandt," I say, "how can you say that, when we see most of the signs you talk about in your book are attributed to an electrical problem?"

He says, "All I can tell you is, that it is not electricity."

"Mr. Schrandt, MSU has tested for every disease that could be causing the immune system to shut down on our cows and there are no diseases present that could cause these problems."

Mr. Schrandt, "All I can tell is that it is not electricity."

"Mr. Schrandt, tell me then when the Primary Neutral in front of our barn was disconnected, where did the electricity go that could no longer go into the ground?"

After the third time I ask this, Mr. Schrandt finally said. "When the electricity could not go down the wire going into the ground in front of barn, it was forced to go back over the wires to the next down ground.", which was at our heifer barn down the road.

I ask, "Mr. Schrandt, is that why the heifers in that barn went from eating 1800# of feed to 800# of feed in three days? They were getting the full effect of more electricity coming to them than had been there before. When that down ground was disconnected, the heifers went back to eating. If the down ground had not been disconnected, the heifers would have starved to death."

Mr. Schrandt said, "All I can tell you is it is not electricity." He would not look us in the eye and he sat there and shook.

We ask him to remove the Primary Neutral in front of our barn and he refused. We ask him if we no longer had cows there if they would take the split-neutral out and he said no. We pleaded with him to help us so that our cows could live. Mr. Schrandt said that they were not going to do anything for us. Finally, I said to him, "Mr. Schrandt, if I have to flip hamburgers at McDonald's, I will fight you and Consumers." They left our farm and went to Victor Mier's and told him the same thing.

The next day, Mr. Schrandt and Bill Hendricks met with a group from the community. The group told them that they believed there was a problem in our community since there had been several farms in the West Branch area over the last several years experiencing the same electrical problems, but the problems had been kept quiet.

I was told after the meeting that anyone who sued Consumers and had been paid out a settlement were under a gag order; They could not talk about what had happened on their farms; the line had been drawn in the sand and Consumers was not going to cross it. Now where do we go for help?

Our community has been very supportive of us, but everyone is busy with their own lives and we have dropped into that black hole. Once you fall into the black hole there does not seem to be a bottom or a way out.

I receive a letter from Representative Dale Sheltrown. He has set up a meeting with the heads of several State agencies for January, 2000. Maybe we can present our case and get someone from the state to help us.

We are facing Y2K and no one knows if the electricity will go down and we will have to generate. Because of the small lines coming into our electrical panel from Consumers, the amount of voltage we pull has caused the small lines from their service to get hot and has caused damage to our box. We need to replace it so we can be ready to generate if we have a power outage on January 1, 2000. We choose, December 30 to replace the disconnect box, and, since Consumers will not come out, we pull the meter ourselves.

While the work is being done, Consumers decides to inspect all the broken down grounds, the empty neutral nut, the mini-substation, the isolators at the curve where the extra neutral lines ends from the school instead of going all the way back to the substation as it should. These are all problems we told Mr. Schrandt about when he was here.

They drove by the farm three times so they could see the work being done on our service. If they would come out, we would not have to remove the meter; work can not be done safely with the meter in place.

We drive to the substation. There are tracks in the snow where I had seen the car parked, so we take some pictures. At the mini-sub, there are tracks also. We then go to the isolators on the curves at the ranch. The tracks indicate that there was a bucket truck there. We wonder what work was done. The inspection seems to have been done at all the locations we told Mr. Schrandt were problems in our area.

Maybe they are finally going to fix the broken down grounds and the insulators that are off the wire and take the tree off the lines. It would be nice if they would start to work with us like Alpena Power did last summer with Mike Timm to relieve the situation, and we could get on with our life.

CHAPTER 13

JANUARY–MARCH 2000

We made it through Y2K. The electricity stayed on with no major blackouts. Our computers still work, as does all of our equipment. We have met a gentleman, Ken Mulholland, who can feel electricity. I would be more doubtful of his ability, if I did not know that my husband, Brian is more sensitive and can also feel the electrical fields.

Mr. Mulholland finds the areas on the farm that are higher in electricity. He puts crushed limestone or chicken grit around the well-head and around the primary neutral which are the lines the utility company uses to place unused electricity in the earth, to find it's way back to the substation. I know that everything that is connected to water—pump, dishwasher, etc. measures more electricity than other circuits.

Chuck Preston our friend who is a retired Agriculture teacher and has some knowledge of the properties of electricity tries to trick Mr. Mulholland, but each time Chuck changes something, Mr. Mulholland feels that it is not right and changes it back. For example, there are certain ways an electric cord on an appliance should be plugged into a wall socket. If the poles are not correct it can cause energy to be omitted that is harmful.

Amazingly, after the chicken grit is applied, the cows turn and face the parlor door and come in on their own some of the time. I wonder how long this will last. I ask Chuck how I am going to know when it is time to put more "magic dust"—crushed limestone around the well and the neutral pole. Chuck agrees that when the cows turn with their tails to the door, put the dust down and see what happens.

We have also installed a water meter to monitor how much water the cows are drinking. Each day Brian measures the gallons of water the cows have drunk to tell us if the amounts vary. The "magic dust" is lasting about ten days. After that time the cows turn away from the parlor doors, so that all I see when I open the doors are tails. After applying the chicken grit around the poles, they turn their heads so they face the parlor doors; I hope it lasts.

We DHIA test and we have the most milk produced (pounds per cow) that we have ever produced. Our cellmatic cell count is the lowest we have ever had. We have bred about 20 cows and they have all become pregnant. Our veterinarian, Dr. Eyth wants to know what has changed. The only change we have made is the "magic dust" around the poles. I hope this improvement continues. If this will work, we could salvage our herd and move on with our life.

Victor and Rose Mier, Brian and I make a trip to Lansing, Representative Dale Sheltrown set up a meeting with about 20 people from various agencies: Dept. of Agriculture, Attorney General, Farm Bureau, and Public Service Commission to discuss our electrical problems on our farms. Vic tells them about what has happened on his farm; sick cows, dead cows, no milk production, etc.

I tell them about what steps we have taken to determine the problem and to ask for specific corrections such as a larger trans-former and upgraded distribution lines. I told them there was enough power from different agencies in that room to correct the problems. They will get back to us to see if there are steps they can take. Some individuals knew there had been numerous voltage problems in the 1990's, but thought the situation had been corrected.

In February, we still have problems with DA's, cows with twisted stomachs, each time we have a drop in water intake of more than three gallons per cow per day; within, one to three days we have a cow with a DA. On one of our silo unloaders, we had a ten horsepower motor burn up the same day we had a drop in water intake. That seems to be a strange coincidence.

People in the community are asking us questions about what is going on at our farm. I think they are concerned it might happen to them. So we decide to have an informational meeting at the Logan Town Hall. We call some people who have asked questions. Within a few days, this meeting has become a big news deal.

The Bay City Times is going to do an article on our farm as well as Vic's farm. As I talk to the reporter, she asks me about a letter written by Dan Wyant, the director of Michigan Department of Agriculture. She indicates that it says we have not worked with the MSU Extension Management Team or availed ourselves of any outside help. I have never seen this letter. She faxes it to me.

She received it from Consumers Energy in an effort on their part to make us look bad. When I received the letter, I notice it is addressed to Vic Mier's brother-in-law. It is in response to a letter he wrote to Governor Engler asking for help for Vic, as well as us, Scott and Frank Bennett.

Mr. Wyant mentions a rule named "Standards of Electrical Service to Customers Having Animals in a Business" which was submitted to the Public Service Commission in April, 1997, and is still waiting for action. He indicates that MSU will help farmers in the area, but that Mr. Mier has not asked for help. The indication from Consumers to the reporter was that none of us had asked for help, and she wanted to know why not? 62

I told her we were under the supervision of the management team headed by Dr. Ron Erskine, and it still was not improving the situation on our farm. The article she writes states most of the facts, but sometimes the reporter gets the farms mixed up, which is a little frustrating.

One of articles in the local paper states that Robert Fisk, MSU Ag. Engineering Department says that the wiring on Vic's farm is not up to code. When asked how he knew that, he had to admit he had never been to the farm. Channel 5 from Bay City has asked if they can do an investigative report on our farm. We are going to present what we have learned to the public at this meeting at the Logan Township Hall.

Channel 5 is going to tape the presentations, as part of their investigative report. Dr. Don Hillman, former MSU professor and Dave Stetzer, an electrician from Wisconsin, are going to be present. Dr. Hillman is going to tell of his research on a number of farms in Michigan and Wisconsin. Dave Stetzer is coming from Wisconsin to show some of his findings from farms where he is collecting data. There is a problem and the public needs to become aware that it is affecting dairy farms across Michigan, and likely going on for a very long time and with no solution on the horizon.

The night before the meeting Dave Stetzer puts the monitoring devices in our milking parlor. We have already installed two copper plates in the floor of the milking parlor to which the wires will be hooked and the lines run to a fluke meter in our office to collect data on harmonics that comes off the parlor floor to be recorded on a computer.

The event meter is already installed in the electrical wall socket to monitor the sags, swells and transients that come from the utility lines. Along with the portalogger that is attached to the primary neutral measuring the voltage going down the neutral wire there is a lot of electrical data being collected.

Along with Dave Stetzer, Don Hillman and Chuck Goeke (who will be doing the statistical work) come to instruct us on the reports we need to complete for them. We now will be keeping track of how many cows from which we put milk into the bulk tank each day. This will tell us if we are losing or gaining milk production as we are taking cows out or adding cows to the herd. This last report will keep a count of dry cows, fresh cows and milk that is not put into the tank for shipment. With all the information we are keeping, it is becoming a full-time job just to keep track of water, feed intake, cow numbers, number of calves fed, milk each day , cow temperatures, sick cows, etc.

In addition to the meetings, we need another way to get more information to the public. I have come up with an idea, like MADD, Mothers against Drunk Driving, so people can learn about our plight. While milking cows, I thought of SAFE (Save Animals From Electricity). I would like to make it a non-profit organization to educate people about the power quality problem and as a support group to help others like us.

I mentioned my idea to Chuck Goeke and that I would like to have a web site. He offered to make a web site for me. God keeps opening the doors!

The next day as I was milking, several men stop at our farm. They have come from down-state to attend the meeting at the Logan Township Hall. One of them told me that it would do no good to try to fight Consumers; he had already done that. He and others had talked to Farm Bureau, their legislators, written letters and basically gone down the same road I was talking about going down. It would not do any good, just be another dead end, but we have to try; maybe if we all hang together we can make a difference.

Channel 5 is here to shoot some footage of the meeting, along with the newspapers. At the hall about one hundred people have shown up to find out more about what is happening on our farms. Several people stand and tell about problems on their farms. There are several attorneys present who have worked on lawsuits against the utility companies. We have several representatives from our legislators at the state and national level.

Maybe we can get more investigations into this problem. Those who have been dealing with this issue for so many years seem to think it will never have a resolution. We must keep trying to move ahead!

Farm Bureau announces that they are going to have a meeting at our house to see what steps can be taken on their part to resolve the gridlock that has occurred. The Attorney General's case which has been setting for five years is soon to come before the Public Service Commission, so things seem to be moving along in a positive direction.

The Bay City Times has another article on the meeting. The more attention we can get the better chance we have to achieve the upgraded distribution lines in our area. Our son, Kevin, called today. He says Paul Harvey had a story about us on his radio show. Mr. Harvey took his information from the Bay City Times article—

March 28, 2000, Cows are walking on tiptoe around Bay City, Michigan. Some are refusing to eat or drink water… On one Prescott farm they buried five cows in one week. Animal health experts could not figure it out but local farmers did. When they noticed the cows picking up their feet…quivering…that was the clue that encouraged local farmers to measure electricity in the ground. And here's how it appears. Rural power lines have deteriorated…at the same time they were being overloaded with new customers…And in the bottlenecks the electricity flows through the ground to complete its circuit. It shocks farm animals. Gradually sickens dairy cows. Officials of the power company say they worked with farmers to rectify stray voltage but they deny it is killing animals and this difference of opinion is now in the courts. The state's Attorney General Frank Kelley says the power company is behaving now like tobacco companies formerly did, denying responsibility. On the Victor Mier farm they pulled the plug on the power company and installed their own generator and their cows are all calm again, eating again, producing again.

How ironic is it that Paul Harvey should pick this topic to talk about on his national show when he was the reason my family moved to Prescott so many years. Life seems to come full circle.

CHAPTER 14

MARCH–JUNE 2000

We have had a good response from the meeting we held at the Logan Township Hall. Channel 5 is still gathering information for the piece; it may be ready this fall. They are being fair and are going to a farm that Consumers has agreed to show them where there are no electrical problems. Seems funny Consumers won't bring them to our farm and prove there are no problems here.

Brian, Vic Mier and Lila Fegan, our township supervisor, stopped at the Michigan Public Service Commission to talk to them about the electrical problems in Ogemaw County. They found that Consumers had cut in half the voltage amounts we are using on our farm. Consumers had submitted the voltage usage making the PSC believe they CE were in compliance.

The weather has turned unusually hot for this time of year and we are experiencing voltage drops below the allowable 114 volts. When this takes place our milking equipment stops and we lose hundreds of pounds of milk down the drain in the floor.

We are also having problems with the cows' health and once again the "magic dust" we thought might be the answer has quit working as well or not at all. The bright spot in all of this is the hearings start on the Attorney General's case against Consumers. Next week we will go to Lansing to see what happens.

At the hearing in Lansing, there are only eight farmers. The hearing is going to be delayed for two weeks because Consumers did not give the AG (Attorney General) the information soon enough. The AG's attorney does take the opportunity to introduce each of us to the Administrative Law Judge. He makes a comment that I am the only woman there. I know that farming is viewed as a man's world and not many women have been involved in the public side of agriculture. It is changing; more women are managing their own farms. There still are prejudices at work. Consumers is having a hard time believing I am serious about what is happening and want a resolution. They think we will just go away.

After the hearing, the farmers are invited to a conference room at the AG's office. It is the first time we have all been together. As we go around the table, farmer after farmer tells their stories. Legs fall off calves on these farms, motors burn up, milk production is down, cows don't drink water, and cows die. The list goes on and on.

It is an eye opening experience to know you are not alone, but no one has been successful in getting Consumers to upgrade large areas. They also talk about the tricks Consumers use on farmers. This is not only illegal for the voltage drops that occur, it is immoral as well. The toll this situation takes on farm families is incredible. Farmers lose their farms due to the economic losses, families are ripped apart by divorce, and farmers lose control and try to kill themselves or their families. For the next hearing we will try to contact more farmers to come and support the Attorney General's office.

The Public Service Commission calls to let us know that they have talked to Consumers and Consumers will be coming to do some testing at our farm. I had just downloaded the portalogger and the voltage has changed. I laughed and said to the PSC, "When did you contact Consumers?"

His answer was, "Last Friday. Why?"

My answer, "Because the voltage changed on Friday. It went to the bottom of the graph instead of the middle. With it measuring less voltage at the bottom, it will make the testing look better."

Locke Mc Greger, (Public Service Commission), "I can't believe that Consumers would do that."

I say, "Well, we are not the ones who control the voltage on the primary neutral. Consumers is."

At the meeting we had at the AG's office, I was given the name of a paralegal who worked for one of the attorney's who had fought Consumers in the past. Unfortunately, he had died, but the paralegal gave me a lot of good insight into how Consumers deals with farmers who have problems. There are some real nightmare stories. One of the tips she gave me was to have a sign-in sheet to keep track of all the people who come to test on your farm. So when Consumers came to do the testing for the PSC, I requested that they sign in. Wow, what a scene.

They would not sign it; it was a legal document according to them, even though I knew it had been used previously. There were calls back and forth with legal counsel and finally they decided not to sign. So no testing was done at that time. Wonders of wonders, within a couple of days the portalogger download measurements were back to the middle of the graph.

The day has finally arrived. It is time to go back to Lansing for the AG's hearings. We have called a lot of farmers, but we don't know if they will show up. So many feel beaten and disheartened. I also set up a news conference, using a list I received from Dale Sheltrown; I fax a notice to the newspapers and several TV stations around Lansing area. And I have placed it in God's hands.

The room is full! Standing room only! There are five TV cameras and nine newspaper reporters there to cover the hearings. I'm having a field day, never having done anything like this before. I am representing all of the people in that room, it's a big responsibility. So I don't want to make any mistakes. All of the attention is a little overwhelming. I have to ask if I'm doing the interviews right. They all say I'm just fine. I must be okay. Consumers calls in two more PR people to make a total of three against just me. The Judge is floored when he sees so many people and cameras.

At one point in the hearing Consumers says that they were not informed of the testing being done on the farms by the AG. The AG's attorney explains that the farmers believe that when Consumers is notified the voltage changes. There is a ripple of laughter in the room. The Judge says any more disturbances and he will clear the courtroom. The farmers have experienced exactly what happened at our farm. The voltages does change when there is going to be testing. We don't know how Consumers does it, but we know it happens.

The Judge decides to proceed with the case. So now the work will begin in earnest. I'm asked if I want to speak to the group before we leave. There are still three Consumer's attorneys in the room, along with the cameras and reporters. I tell the group, "that we are not fighting Consumers alone; we now have the state of Michigan fighting with us and God's on our side." The three Consumers attorneys stand there looking at the floor, hopefully in shame. It was a good day.

Back home we have a meeting with the MSU Management Team.

They have been monitoring us since last October. They have noticed the interval we had in January, when everything went very well. We have been told by the County agent before the meeting, they will not discuss anything electrical. So when I was asked what happened, I say, "We can't talk about electricity." Dr. Erskine insists knowing what happened! I explain about the "magic dust", how it worked and then did not, much to our disappointment. They know nothing else changed. They have the records to prove that. They also have no answers as to why we keep having DA's and other problems. They will continue to monitor and another date for a meeting will be set up.

Consumers has an annual meeting the last Friday in May. We decide to attend. They have a large presentation on all of the new investments they have made overseas in Africa, Indonesia and Venezuela. They have a question and answer time and I ask "When are they going to upgrade the distribution lines that run in front of our house?"

The CEO, Mr. McCormmick talks about "stray voltage" and how farmers do their own wiring. And the problems on farms are caused by the farmers. I guess we will just have to keep coming to annual meetings until we get an answer. When are they going to upgrade our lines?

The Attorney General's office has made arrangements to have testing done on our farm. They set the equipment on a Wednesday and don't tell Consumers until the following Monday. Will wonders never cease? The portalogger measurements changed to the bottom of the graph on Monday.

We now know through information the AG received that Consumers uses a program from Cymdist that gives them the ability to change the voltages on the lines. While the voltage is down all is ok. But when it spikes, the cows react. They fall down in the parlor. They drink seven point two gallons less water.

We call Consumers back and show them the graphs and the other testing equipment in our parlor. We beg them to help us; to make the changes that Alpena Power had made at Mike Timms by moving the primary neutral away from the barn. Consumers do not like the test results from the AG's test. They disagree with the low voltage of 106.9, well below the allowable limit of 114 volts.

Consumers decides to do their own testing after a week in which we had the vacuum pump turn off so many times that we generated our own electricity by a portable generator to finish several milkings. The test results from Consumers were a low of 107. I asked them if that was any where close to the 106.9 the week before results?

One report showed that 162 times during the week of Consumers own testing our voltage went below the 114 volt allowable limit. We now have conclusive results that we have a power quality problem on our farm and Consumers chooses to ignore it.

We have already lost twenty-two cows this year and fifty-eight last year. We have less than a hundred cows left. We make a huge decision; we will sell our cows as soon as possible. It will be a major life altering change for us. Summer is our worst time with all the additional usage on our substation.

We meet with Farm Credit, our mortgage holder, and they okay the sale. This decision has huge ramifications for us. We have spent most of our lives growing up on farms. We have been here in Prescott on Nansue Farms since 1966. Our mission statement states what we have tried to live by for thirty-four years:

> Our mission is to produce a superior product by wisely using our resources. We strive to achieve for both the family and employees a standard of living that allows us to enjoy a balance of work and leisure time, while maintaining efficiency. We take pride in being leaders in use of new technology as it and monetary resources become available, in owning land and well kept

machinery, in producing quality feed, with the result being the production of quality milk that makes us an asset to our community and the dairy industry. We humbly accept these responsibilities as God has given us to carry out.

Nansue Farms, Brian and Nancy Bellville

For us to have to give up our dairy herd is devastating. We are going to be faced with a future full of questions. How will we survive? How will we produce an income? Yet the decision to sell our cows was unavoidable. We could not keep them SAFE. It is not fair to subject them to such unneeded suffering and even death. So we must get them away from this environment. It breaks my heart to have to let them go, but we must think of what is best for our animals and put the rest in God's hands. The sale is set for August 7, 2000.

CHAPTER 15

JUNE 2000

When we make the decision to sell our cows, we meet with Farm Credit. In 1966 we started with Farm Credit, an organization started in the last 1930's to loan money to farmers, so we have dealt with them for an awful lot of years. In the 1970's we built our milking parlor and our free stall barns. The loan officer in charge told us later that he had his doubts that we could make it. He watched us for years and said we always did what we told them we were going to do.

The 1980's found life tight for farmers when land prices dropped and interest rates hit twenty percent. Over night the farmers found themselves with no equity, due to the drop in land value. Farms were repossessed. Many farmers could not take the life change and committed suicide. Also, some farmers were given deals to write down part of their debts when times got bad. We have always been able to pay our way. It has been a good working relationship.

Farm Credit has agreed that we can sell the cows and they will work with us to switch things around so we can keep the farm. We will have to raise more steers, fatten them and sell them for the meat market. We will sell our excess crops. The mortgage will have to be redone, as we will no longer have the monthly income for the payments, and we will need more years to pay it off.

We would have had most of our debt paid off in five years. Now we will take a step back, but it should be okay. We already raise our steers for beef and have sold our excess crops; there will just be more of them because the cows will not be there to eat the feed. We will raise bottle babies, calves two to three days old, until they reach 1200-1400pounds and sell them for beef. It will take us about two years to accomplish this and get a rotation.

Because the summer is our worst time, due to the heat, we have set our sale as soon as possible, July 8, 2000. We have a lot to do in a short time. Because of the TB issue in Michigan, each animal over one year of age has to be tested, which only gives us three weeks. So we test. The animals are put into a chute with a head lock; they put their heads through bars and are locked around the neck. They are identified by an ear tag and given a shot under the tail. It takes us about six hours and eight people to accomplish this task. Several of our neighbors help us. We are told that cows under stress can test positive. Then three days later we do it again. It's quite a job.

The test results come in and we have about twenty animals that are suspect and will have to be tested again. The State veterinarian comes and we retest those animals with a shot in the neck this time. Their neck is measured and the shot administered. In three days the neck is measured again, and if there is swelling then they will be considered positive. Four animals come back positive. They will have to be sent to Lansing, killed and tested. The test will have to go to Iowa. Until the results come back, we are under quarantine.

There will be no sale for a while. It is a real mess to cancel and reschedule the sale. Everyone is really nice and understanding about it. There probably is no problem, but the State has to be sure there are no diseases present.

Emotionally we are on a roller coaster. All of our dreams; all of the land that we have bought, cleared, and improved over the years. All the hard work that we have spent thirty-five years doing is in jeopardy. The years we have spent on improving the animals, going from 13,000 pounds of milk to 21,000 pounds; the joy of raising animals that came in first at the Fairs or gave us local DHIA records in our county; all of this will be gone because Consumers Energy would not fix a problem they are aware is harming our animals and causing our equipment to malfunction. If they would have worked with us like Alpena Power worked with the farmer up North, we could have continued to milk our cows, improve their genetics, work the land until we would retire and give the reins to someone else.

Now Nansue Farms will no longer exist as we had built it. There is so much of us in this farm. The sweat equity, the insurmountable hours that our family spent making this a respected entity; all of our memories. We knew where we wanted to go and what we wanted to accomplish. We had it all mapped out. All of that is destroyed. What does the future hold for us? How do we continue? I am so sad and scared!

CHAPTER 16

JULY 2000

We have been invited to attend a conference at a farm in Coopersville, Michigan. Dave Stetzer from Wisconsin will be there. He is going to do some electrical testing at the same time as Consumers. There are several newspaper and TV crews at the conference. Don Hillman presents some of his findings of testing done on farms in Michigan and Wisconsin.

We meet Dr. Martin Graham, from California, for the first time. He says that over the years the electrical usage has changed to non-linear loads: TV's, hairdryers, computers, microwaves, and the like. All of these appliances use 110 volts and so the electrical loads are not balanced any longer.

Consumers pull in with an entourage of about ten cars. It looks like a scene out of a movie. They refuse lunch and won't even have a can of pop. All of a sudden things erupt, Consumers is demanding the raw data from some testing Dave Stetzer did on this farm the day before and earlier this morning.

In April at the hearing, it had been agreed that Consumers and Stetzer would both set up and test. Then the raw data would be exchanged. Now Consumers wants Stetzer's before they do any testing. The head attorney from Consumers, Jim Brenum, is nose to nose with Stetzer, arguing about the farm testing. Finally I say to them if they need a farm to test, Consumers had agreed in writing to test with both of them present on our farm. All of a sudden, they decide to do some testing on this farm.

Once again, it is only hand-held equipment. And watching the measurements over their shoulders, the measurements they are giving to be written down are less than what the meter reads. Is this the game Consumers plays, always using measurements less than they are really getting? They are not too happy with all of us keeping an eye on them. As the day wears on and more people come home from school and work, the voltage readings start to go up and about 5:00 p.m. Consumers suddenly decides they can't do any more testing. They will have to wait and come back in the morning. Why does that not surprise me? Consumers never will test if it looks like the voltage readings will not be in their favor.

Last summer when I had told my son about the Harmonics, he said he had studied about that for Mechanical Engineering and it was bad stuff. He wanted me to talk to his Professor which I had tried to do.

Now Professor Parks, who was recommended to us, is working for Consumers. He must be good. They have made sure he could not help us, just like the Veterinarian Dr. Sanders from Ohio that Consumers paid over $1,000,000 to work for them.

As we talked to Professor Parks on the side and told him our situation, he said we had a problem. Consumers was upset that we talked to him. They told us to stay away from him. Stetzer is upset with how the testing was handled. It did not go as the judge in April had ordered.

CHAPTER 17

AUGUST 2000

As the days linger, we go with the routine. The sale has now been set for August 7, 2000. The test results are back, and there is no TB. The quarantine is lifted. The crew from the sale firm who will hold the auction of the cattle and the milking equipment are here. They set up the gates, the tent, and sort the cattle.

Channel 11 will be here with a film crew to do a news cast on our sale. And the reporter from Detroit Free Press is here for an interview. He has been very good in keeping to the facts. Sometimes he has gotten our farm and Vic and Rose Mier's farms mixed up, but for the most part he did not get creative.

It is good that many people will know that there is a problem that needs to be addressed. The reporters and news people have many questions. How does it feel to have to sell your cows? What are you going to do in the future? Are you going to sue Consumers Energy? How do you know it is their fault? How do I answer the questions when I feel like I have fallen down Alice in Wonderland's hole?

The last few days have been unreal. Today is the sale. We milk the cows after midnight so that the cow's udders will be full of milk and look good at sale time. Then they will be milked as they are sold. Kay, our daughter, will be in the parlor with our hired man. The sale crew will move the cows and other animals. The sale will start at noon, High noon, like in the movie. It feels the same way: a show down.

I have to do this; Brian is not good at talking, so that job will be mine. God, please help me. Give me the words I need to say to make people understand. We start the sale. The auctioneer introduces Brian and me to the crowd. There are about 100-150 people. He then asks me to say a few words.

I say that we have farmed here for thirty-five years. We have had a good herd of cows. I hold the plaque that we were awarded for three cows who were the top milk producers in the county at the time. We are the only ones to have three animals on it. Our herd has been good to us, but we have an electrical problem on the farm and as Consumers will not help us, it is in the best interest of our animals to sell them and get them out of this environment.

I know they have the ability to produce more than we can get out of them. We have removed those animals that had any problems. The rest of the herd is sound. I thank them for their support.

The auctioneers now take over to sell our animals. We are having a video made of the sale. I stay for a little while, but I just can't watch the animals I have raised go through the ring. So many memories; the cows that we watched be born or helped to be born. The cows we watched grow up and start to produce milk. The joy of having a cow come up to have her head scratched while you were watching the feed go out to the cows on the elevator. Looking out in the exercise dry lot and seeing cows lying down contented to chew their cud; of snow storms, when it took all day just to clear the yards of snow so we could feed the animals; or all the cement we poured ourselves to build all of these barns that will sit empty.

I remembered how my kids played outside the barn in the sand box while I milked, or sat on the steps in the milking parlor; the hours we shared milking and discussing the events of the day in school, uninterrupted time to share our thoughts, or, as in my son's case, tried to talk me into buying him a new truck.

Many good times and trying times come to mind as I watch a chapter come to a close in our lives. I am not sure I'm ready for the next chapter to start; I'd like to cling to the past a little longer.

All too soon the sale is over, and the animals are loaded. The reporters have been talked to. The TV cameras are gone. The crew has cleaned up. The crowd is gone and so are the cows. It's so quiet. I can't walk through the empty barns. We still have our steers, but it is so lonely. It's not the same when it's milking time and there are no sounds. It only takes about an hour to get our chores done now. Kay likes it because she doesn't have as much work to do, but then she's only twelve years old.

So many hours to fill that never were a problem, so many things to ponder. Did we make the right move? What does the future hold?

Are we going to make it? So many questions, very few answers, so many worries, so many doubts!

CHAPTER 18

September–December 2000

After selling the cows, life settles into a very non-descriptive existence. The days are long. We never had enough time to do all the things that needed to be taken care of and now, there are so many hours to fill in a day. I also know why the cash crop farmers, those who only raise oats, wheat, corn, sugar beets, soybeans, no cattle, go to the coffee shop every day.

There are no more people coming to see us. Every day we had the milkman, feed salesmen, breed salesmen or the veterinarian come to our farm to talk to. Now the phone is silent and we see no one. It feels like we have dropped off the face of the earth.

I can understand what it's like when you quit smoking. The longing, the fix you need. You miss that interaction with people! We have been such a part of the community for so long; it feels like a part is missing. The farming community thinks we don't care about what is going on. The price of milk has dropped, and everyone tells us we're so lucky not to have to worry about it. People think we should be happy not to have all the work and worry about the price of milk and feed. I'd give anything to have my healthy cows back!

The feelings we are experiencing are the same as when someone dies. We are grieving for a way of life we knew for more than fifty years. Nansue Dairy Farm died the day we sold the cows. There are support groups that you can go to when people die. We have to do this on our own, especially when we have the electricity issue thrown in. No one wants to go there! I know what a widow feels like when she's not included in all the activities that were once part of a life together as a couple.

The only thing that is getting us through is that we are in it together.

And we have Vic and Rose Mier to talk to; they still have their cows and are still trying to deal with the electricity issue by generating their own electricity.

Farm Credit has not given us the money to fill the barn with steers so we can switch over to raising steers and cash crops. They control all the money from the sale of the cows. When I ask for some to pay the feed bill, they refused. They are supposed to pay the monthly payments out of that money. They had agreed to pay the feed bill also.

Thank goodness we had some money from the sale of some cull cows so I could pay all the outstanding bills. But we need to be able to have money to live until we can get a rotation of cattle going to have an income.

This is going to be a challenge getting the financial end worked out. Our payments were on a monthly basis. With no monthly income, we need to switch things to annual payments and redo our debt to make the payments match our income. Farm Credit had promised to work with us, when we met to sell the cows.

We meet with the head of the Farm Land Preservation; they are a state group with money to buy development rights so that the land will not be sold for anything except farming. We must hurry to get all the paper work done and sent into the State. They will be picking some farms to buy the development rights; this is the amount of money our farm is worth to someone outside of agriculture to build houses or develop in some way. If we could get this, we could pay Farm Credit off and continue to farm. We only have a few weeks to get all this turned in and there are so many hoops to jump through.

We receive a foreclosure notice from Farm Credit. It seems they forgot to tell us they could not use the money in escrow to pay the land payment. We either have to come up with a lot of money or they are going to take the farm. Where is the help they were going to give us? We must meet with them to see what we can work out.

Two guys from Farm Credit meet with us, our loan officer, and the Credit Risk manager who grew up in Prescott. The meeting does not go well; the Credit Risk manager wants us to sell our machinery. If we sell that, we might as well sell the land too, because we will not have equipment to work the fields, to raise and harvest crops that would provide money to pay our debt. This is a pretty hard sell.

Where is the cooperation they were going to give us? Our loan officer is not saying anything. He was the one who agreed to work with us. After meeting a couple of times and not getting anywhere by ourselves, we call in MSU extension to meet with them. The minute it is mentioned that we might need an attorney, the attitude changes. They will work something out. We manage to make up all the payments for the rest of the year by using the last milk check. That check was going to be our income for the next year.

We also buy seven steers to add to what we already have, but it's not going to be enough to make it. We just bought a little time. Things must be worked out in order for us to continue.

Farm Land Preservation notifies us that they are not interested in preserving our land. They are using the money to preserve land around Kalamazoo and Traverse City. They don't feel land north of Bay City is worth saving yet. That is too bad; there are very few pieces with 740 acres all in one piece.

We spent thirty-five years putting the land together. The first piece we bought was in 1966, a 120 acres across the road from my parents farm. My folk's farm was next. Another piece was added next to the first 120 acres. Eighty acres sat for seven years before we could put it in. Then the man responsible for an estate of another eighty acres came to us and asked if we wanted to buy it. They would clear the estate which had set unsettled for twenty plus years. We added forty acres that my parents wanted to sell, and the last 160 acres came to us out of the blue. It's good land, some of the best farmland in Ogemaw County. Now it is at risk.

Farm Credit says we have to sell some of it. It is easy for them to want to sell the land. They have nothing invested in it except money. My kids, Brian and I cleared some of the acreage which was into woods, picked the stones and junk off it. We leveled the ditches, and took out the fence rows and trees to make it the nice, clear uninterrupted land it is today. One field could be a mile long. We have road frontage for one mile on one side, a half mile on the other, and one whole section except for forty acres. It seems such a shame to have to split it up.

It has become known we may have to sell some land and a girl who grew up in this area is looking for some land to build a house so they can move here. The piece they want is not one we really want to sell, but we have to do something. It's a piece in the middle of the 1 mile section, but it's the hardest piece to work as it has several bunches of trees in it. It is a good price and it will satisfy Farm Credit for a while.

It is the hardest thing to do after selling the cows. It seems like the beginning of the end. I have shed a lot of tears over it, but we don't have any choice. Maybe if we do this, Farm Credit will see we are trying and will cooperate to keep us in business.

Farm Credit has waited until the 28th of December to redo our note. We have to sign the papers or be in default again. This will get our operating money for next year. Still no cattle but they are supposed to get that done soon, so we can start to fill the barns.

The year 2000 is closing and so many changes have occurred. I know selling the cows was the right thing to do. They needed to leave the electrical environment that was causing them so much stress and health problems. But I really miss them. I miss the life we had revolving around them. I miss the people we met through them. I miss the hustle and bustle of what our life was like for thirty-five years. I'm still grieving for all of those things, and yet I know we must move on. It's just easier said than done.

The future is still uncertain with a lot of questions yet unanswered. But our faith in God will always get us through wherever the path goes that we are going to follow.

Chapter 19

We start the year with the sale of the forty acres. We don't want to get rid of any acreage, but Farm Credit is really leaning on us. By selling this, we can put the money on our loan and get it in line. I still cry a lot. We have worked so hard putting this farm together and to sell part of it is very difficult to accept. I try to adjust to the upheaval going on in our daily life.

Farm Credit has changed our payment back to annual instead of monthly, thank goodness. But we still need to lengthen it out so our annual payment will match our income. That is one of the hardest things to handle.

Payments, equipment, daily routine has changed so much. It takes time to pull all of it in line again. And we still do not have the cattle in the barns that we need. If Farm Credit doesn't allow us to get cattle in soon, it is going to be very difficult to meet our obligations. It seems like we traded one set of problems with sick cows for another, trying to get things adjusted. It seems never ending.

Brian, Vic and Rose Mier, and I make a trip to Wisconsin to Dave Stetzer's home.

We spend time going over a lot of literature that Dave has on the effects of electricity on the human body. Dave says that the electricity coming into the houses adversely affects people.

We met a lady who had been a social worker, but had to quit because she could not function. Her memory was so bad that she could not remember her sisters' names or to eat. Within a couple of days after Dave put filters on her house, she could remember things. When we met her she had improved—not totally, but she could function again.

I believed her because the summer of 1999 when things were so bad for our cows, I had trouble remembering things. I thought

I was coming down with Alzheimer's, and I was scared to death. We also met Kurt Gutknecht who wrote several articles on Dirty Electricity. I wanted to meet Chris Hardy, who also wrote articles on electricity, but we could not make it happen.

We met with John Beyrel. His story was like the rest. He had one of the top herds in the nation. John had a tie stall barn and was spending all of his time in the barn. So they built a new parlor and barn and then their problems started. He has not been able to get the utility company to do anything for him.

We stopped to visit one of the guys on the Select Sires-MABC board with Brian who lives just about eight miles from the Beyrel's. He has an older barn and he told us he was afraid to build new because he was doing well and he did not want the same thing to happen to him that happened to the Beyrel's. It really is funny how you can travel two states and have people say the same thing.

In our area, people don't want to talk about it because it might happen to them. I'm not sure what the answer is or when the problem might get resolved.

Wisconsin has had problems just like Michigan and continues to fight with the utility companies. But we met with one utility company, Jackson Electric Cooperative, Black River Falls, Wisconsin. The manager there told us that they had farmers who complained about "stray voltage," and they built new grounded lines to these farms. After they built the lines, the milk production went up on each of the farms on the line.

One farmer joked they cost him money because he had to buy a bigger tank for his milk to fit into. It would really be nice if Consumers would work that hard to remedy the problems they are having on Michigan farms instead of thinking farmers are expendable.

Mike Timm is doing fine after Alpena Power moved his Primary Neutral away from his barns. I wish we could have worked together and been able to keep our cows.

We have filed a lawsuit against Consumers Energy for the damages on our farm. After the calculations were done we have lost or will lose over three million dollars. Now the process starts in the legal system. All we ever wanted to do was raise our kids, milk cows and retire someday. All of those dreams and plans

Brian and I had made disappeared like a poof of smoke. Hard work had always kept us in control. Now we have no control over what is happening in our life and it is pretty frightening. It felt like Alice in Wonderland's tunnel. When you land, it is in a different place. We have to fight and not give up.

Farm Bureau goes to Washington every year and meets with the legislators. This year we are going to talk to legislators about the electrical problem. Our daughter, Lori and her husband live in Arlington, Virginia, so we can stay with them. We have appointments with about 15 staff members. It is very difficult to see the Congressmen themselves. All of the staff members are very sympathetic and can't believe that electricity is hurting cows and destroying farms.

We meet with someone from Senator Feingold's (Wisconsin) office. They are aware of the electrical problems since Wisconsin has a lot of problems like Michigan. Some of the electrical companies over there work with the farmers and correct the problems on farms while others are like Consumers and think farms and farmers are expendable. We meet with Kim Love from Debbie Stabenow's office, they have been very helpful. There is some talk of doing an energy policy. Vice President Chaney is heading an investigation on energy hopefully they will look at electricity not just fuel.

Farm Bureau has arranged to meet with different legislators; it's pretty interesting when some of them recognize you, that is good maybe they will keep us in mind in the future. Maybe they will remember and ask questions when the energy subject comes up.

At one of our meetings, we had a speaker named, Andrew Lindquest, who happened to be in charge of the Energy task force for Vice-President Chaney. He told us that Arizona pulls energy from all four corners of the state and loses enough off the transmission lines to supply California with all the electricity they need. I got the chance to ask him, "Our national transmission and distribution system is so antiquated, did he think we would every get upgraded, so that the excess electricity that goes into ground could be put on a wire?"

His answered that he was aware of the antique line problem and that he hoped that would be one of the things they would look at in reference to electricity. That sounds hopeful! All and all it was a productive trip. At least we have made contacts in Washington that we can use in the future.

We have some new experiences, riding the subway by ourselves is challenging. Never having experienced city life, underground in a subway was disconcerting. We are used to wide open spaces. But after three days we learn our way around. Big city life still is not for me but it sure was nice to spend time with Lori and Brian.

Coming home on an upbeat was good, but it does not help with the situations in the real world. Vic and Rose Mier have decided to sell their cows.

They had problems with their herd before us, and it was the discussion of their problems that led us to discover what was wrong with our herd of cows.

They were the first to have the Attorney General in our area, the first to tackle Consumers and try to get them to fix the problem. Mier's tried a lot of different things to relieve the electrical influence on their farm. Vic used an Agrivolt system that balances the load, by encircling the farm with irrigation pipe to chase the voltage in the ground away from the buildings. After a year of relief, as with many of the other fixes, the comfort that the cows got from not having electricity affecting them is gone and the results of electrical influences has returned.

Vic and Rose are tired of fighting sick cows and the utility company. The whole community is at the sale, some to offer support, some out for a deal. It brings back memories of our sale. Life as we all knew it is gone!

Those who have supported Mier's, Brian and I will never know how much it has meant to have people who believe all the problems are not your fault or that you are not crazy.

Successful Farming, a national farm magazine, published an article by Cheryl Tevis about the Mier's and us. As a result of the article, I started to receive phone calls from all over the country from people having the same problems we were having on our farm. We heard from Virginia, Pennsylvania, New York, Missouri, Wisconsin, Minnesota, Oregon, and Washington.

A farmer in New York had the same problem with his John Deere 8200 tractor as we did. When the tractor goes over an electrical field that runs through the ground returning the electricity back to the substation and the tractor meters go crazy. It interferes with the hydraulics, it deadens batteries, and makes the fuel gauges read full when they are empty.

One lady (Wendy) told me about moving back to her husband's home farm. She started to feel ill; everyone said she was just upset. There were certain places on the farm where she felt worse. Then after a while her two year old daughter developed arthritis. She had gotten to the point of not being able to walk very well and the doctors had her on the highest dose of medicine. The woman remembered that when her daughter left the farm she felt better, so she sent her to live with her sister for a while.

Since her sister lived a long ways from them, they could not see the girl everyday. After two weeks when they visited her, the daughter could walk to them. When she was tested by the doctors after a month her levels were normal again. They are now looking for a place to live away from the farm.

There were stories of people not being able to use part of their homes because they felt so bad in one part of the house. Some slept on the floor in the living room instead of in the bedrooms. Beyrel's had told us about the same thing at their house and how they deflected the ground current. We have experienced waking up at 3:00 a.m. every night and can not seem to find what wakes us up.

A farmer in Virginia called. He has sued his utility company and they have set up a visit to his farm. One of the people coming will be Dr. Sander from Ohio. How small a world is it, the same people rotate around the country on both side of the issue.

An Amish farmer called from Missouri. He had problems and the utility company down there told him they could not be causing him any problems because he was not connected to them. When the electricity comes through the ground, it does not matter whether you are hooked to the utility or not.

The utility companies do not want to accept responsibility for the electricity they put into the ground and the rest of us can not do anything about it. So farmers will keep going out of business and the general public will continue to have health issues.

Chapter 20

We finally got some money to start buying steers, not enough to fill the barn, but enough to get a start. With having to buy baby calves, it will take us a couple of years to get enough for a rotation. Farm Credit still is not doing any thing to bring our payments into line, so we still have the financial worry hanging over our head.

Life is settling down to some kind of a routine. It only takes a couple of hours to do chores and then the rest of the day can be spent on field work. It seems funny not to have to stop at 4:00 p.m. and go milk cows. It is lonesome after having had people come to the farm everyday.

People in the area who have cows say we are lucky because the price of milk has dropped, but I'd give anything to have my cows back. Channel 7 (out of Detroit) flew the Attorney General Jennifer Granholm up to look at a site on Henderson Lake road. It was nice to meet her and she was very personable. She had attended the funeral of Richard Austin (long time Michigan Secretary of State) and had flown directly to West Branch airport and she brought her daughter with her. The guys from her office hooked one end of a wire to the down ground and measured about 14 volts going from the pole into the earth.

They hooked the other end to a wire fence to ground it and hooked that to a train car. The volt was enough to move the car around the track. If you changed the wire it ran the car backwards. Then they hooked the wire to three rockets and there was enough heat from the wire to heat the fuel cell on each rocket and blast them twenty feet in the air.

The day before they had run a TV off the voltage from the down ground, but the voltage had been at 20 volts. They then illuminated an arrow sign. They ask Attorney General Granholm if this voltage was dangerous. She said that there was twenty times the amount it would take to stop a human heart going down the pole into the ground.

A few neighbors stopped by to see what was going on and were really surprised to watch all the things that happened. Hopefully, Attorney General Granholm can help us somewhere down the road. She already has by getting the hearings going against Consumers Energy.

The week after we did the testing at Henderson Lake road, I downloaded the portalogger. I found out why the voltage was lower the day the Attorney General was up. The men from her office had been there the day before her visit and tested. They measured 20 volts and ran a TV. As luck would have it, someone from Consumers Energy saw them and asked them what they were doing.

As I downloaded the portalogger, I discovered that within two hours of the time Consumers talked to them the voltage raised on our side of the substation, so it should have lowered on the other side which goes up to Henderson Lake road.

As the days of fall come, we have heard on our lawsuit, pages and pages of interrogatories (questions about anything and everything). I spent time making a history of all the things that have happened to us since 1998.

From what other people who have sued Consumers before tell us, Consumers tries to make the farmer look bad. After all your cows are sick, milk production is down and too many of animals are dying, they blame it on poor management.

Farmers tend to blame themselves and Consumers feeds on those feelings. The turmoil the farm and the farm family are dealing with can place tremendous stress on marriages. Fifty percent of farm families involved in electrical problems end up divorcing. Brian and I are in this together, so hopefully we will beat the odds.

Kay (our only child home) likes having more free time. She can go to horse shows and do some other things the other kids could not do because we were so busy. But I found an essay she wrote for school that surprised me, I did not know the depth of her feeling. This is what she wrote:

The World of Black and White

To some, caring for dairy cows is a way of life. That was the way it was for my family and me, before the stray voltage problems with Consumer's Energy started. For fifteen years of my life, I was used to living on a dairy farm. That meant waking up at 5:00 in the morning and normally working until dark. The farm was a part of the family, and everyone was involved in the farm. Most of my memories from when I was younger are from the farm. Dairy farming was a hard life, but there was something that I just loved about it.

Our way of living unexpectedly began to change when I was thirteen. My parents started having trouble with the cows and younger heifers. The cows would not have calves and if they did calve, they would not produce as much milk as they should. At the time, we had a lot of sick cows. They would get sick for no justification. Even the baby calves, such innocent little creatures, would drop dead like flies for no apparent reason.

My parents sought help from local vets. Eventually, they had vets from Michigan State University, which is one of the top five universities for Veterinary Medicine in the US, try to solve the problems. They used the best medicines, vaccinations, and feed rations. The care for the cows became so tedious that we knew how much water each cow would drink everyday. Sadly, we had one of the best cared for dairy herds around, but the problems with our cattle persisted.

Two years later, we found out why the cows were so sick. Some other dairy farmers in the area were having similar problems with their cows. They found that their problems were caused by stray voltage in the ground. The stray voltage depleted the immune systems of the cows. With depleted immune systems, common, easily cured illnesses became life threatening. The cow's bodies could not take any stress.

Furthermore, the cows would not eat or drink because they would get an electrical shock when they touch the feeders. Through extensive testing, they then concluded through research that Consumers Energy, which is the local supplier for electricity, was found the cause.

Some people do not believe that there is such a thing as stray voltage because it is invisible to the human eye and so hard to understand that most of the time only a person that is trained in the field of electricity can understand it.

Hearing about the problems on other farms, my parents decided to investigate our farm for a similar problem. They met with a man that worked for Consumers Energy to see if they would check on the farm to make sure that stray voltage was not the issue. For a while, we worked with Consumers Energy to try figure out what could be done to save the cows from the deadly electricity that would cause them to literally starve to death.

He explained how there was no way that stray voltage could have any effect on the cattle. My parents did not agree. They contacted the Michigan Attorney General to see if there is any way to do more extensive testing. An independent firm tested on our farm and found that there was a deadly amount of stray voltage.

That summer, with many cattle dying, my parents decided that it was best for the cows to be sold to safer homes. Neither my mother nor my father wanted to end thirty-five years of dairy farming.

They decided to sell the cattle that were under the most stress and that were most vulnerable to stray voltage. They sold the milking cows and all of the female cattle. My parents decided to keep all of the steers and to raise and sell them when they were ready for market. During the time of the sale, my parents were very stressed. They got a lot of attention from the media including news stations and newspapers.

After the sale, life was much different. The sale of the cows changed my daily routine. Now I have more time to do other things that my siblings were never able to do. Although I have more time, the farm is not the same with the empty, lifeless barns that were once filled with black and white Holsteins.

When I found this essay and read it. I cried, I thought we had protected her from some of the hurt. I found out just how deep the cut runs in families that become involved in this issue. Even the kids are not protected or sheltered.

One lady told me that the utility company "breaks your spirit and you never get it back." No matter what the future brings I will never let the utility company take that away from me. I will fight for those who have lost their farms, families, spent time in jail as a result of this and for all of the bitter and spirit-broken families.

I am learning that the only way I can deal with this is to place it in God's hands and pray for direction as what to do next. This is the hardest lesson to learn and the biggest promise to keep. In July of 1999, when we had five cows die, I prayed for God to help us. We could not do this alone.

I promised I would write a book; little did I know what a journey this would be and I have no idea what the future holds. I only know God will be with us every step of the way and things will unfold His way and in His time We did not have long to wait for things to start to happen!

CHAPTER 21

OCTOBER–DECEMBER 2001

Another farm in our area has decided to sell their cows. This farm had electrical problems in the past, sued Consumers Energy, was paid money, and had a gag order placed on them. Little was known about their case. They have started to talk a little. They believe that the voltage is back and affecting their cows. Last time they had family health problems and they just don't want to have to deal with this again. I don't blame them. Now they will change their lives totally.

We are learning a little about the health effects that electricity has on people. It is scary and unbelievable that these can happen and the utility company does not have to be accountable. There have been many (over 300 studies done in Eastern Europe) that used real people. They all showed that there is a problem when a human comes under the influence of an EMF field. Each farm I talked to that has sick animals have people that are sick too.

Our neighbor who had cancer previously, took straw off one of the fields that we had identified as having pathways in it. She spent three days chopping the straw and with in a week her cancer had come back. The doctors told her the cancer came from an environmental source. She lives within a quarter of a mile of a high line (distribution line), and the doctors told her she needed to move. She has a farm and how does she get rid of all she has worked so hard to achieve?

The land that we sold has a house built on it now. And there are two pathways now; I don't know why the second one came, one on each side of the house. The family finally moved into the house and the wife developed breast cancer within two weeks of moving into the house.

She had just had a check up that did not show any problem. It certainly happened fast. If you have a health problem, does the electricity make it worse? You just have to wonder!

My husband Brian has to have a procedure done on his heart to correct an irregular heart beat. While we are in the hospital watching the news, the investigative report Channel 5 has spent many months putting together was showing. They really did a nice job of telling both sides of the story.

Not only did Channel 5 come up to our farm and our area, Consumers Energy take them to a farm they wanted them to see. Channel 5 asked them to come to our farm and test, but Consumer's Energy declined. They had a farm chosen to test. That didn't surprise me. This is the third time they have declined to come to our farm. If there is not a problem, why are they so afraid to test here and prove us wrong? The Channel 5 team asked that question and (got the usual run around.) Consumers will not publicly do testing on any farm. They choose farms they know will test well.

On this other farm Consumer's Energy ran tests in the water the cows drank to show that there was no voltage in the water. It would have been interesting to have them test the same places on our farm, because we have tested the water in our barn. The cows stand there and lap water before they finally will dip their nose into the water, and every time the strobe lights trip on the communication tower (that is Consumer's Energy) you can measure it in our barn.

December 10, 2001 is another red letter day. Three years to the day from when Consumer's Energy came to our door, they came back to test. Pretty ironic! The whole crew, Dr. Stringfellow-Arizona, Dr. Aneshansley-Cornell, Mr. De Nardo, Mr. Dagenhart, Drs. Albright, Bancroft, and Lane, they descend as usual, along with Consumer's attorney Michael Reynolds.

Mr. De Nardo and Mr. Dagenhart measured the down grounds in the area. Low and behold, they found several broken down grounds. They even found some we did not know about. They also found two broken insulators. All of these can affect the quality of electricity. We have been telling them for three years that there were broken down grounds, showed them pictures. They just don't believe us.

Drs. Albright, Bancroft, and Lane spent all day measuring each and every free stall (the partition that separates each cow and forms an area for them to lie down in). When you get 1500-2000 pound cows bumping or pushing on the free stalls, they have a tendency to move a little, even though they are bolted in place, so it was funny watching them measure each one to see if they could say "all of our problems were due to bad free stalls." As I have said before, I counted cows and we put new free stalls in to see if it made any difference. It did not! They would always lie in the smallest free stall in the barn.

Dr. Aneshansley spent the day measuring the amount of voltage on each drinker on the farm. When they got to the barn that we had taken the video of the heifer stepping, the voltage on those drinkers was higher and they were not hooked to any electricity!

Dr. Aneshansley kept saying, "Are you sure there isn't any electricity here?" The higher voltage had to be coming through the earth. He could not explain where it was coming from. Of course no one would let them talk to us.

Dr. Stringfellow spent the day doing electrical measurements. Of course, no one would measure the voltage in the earth!

About ten days after Consumer's Energy visited our farm, they came back in to repair the down grounds and the insulators. They went two miles around us on the next road, instead of going by our house to fix the broken down ground that was on our road about a half a mile east of our house. That way they did not have to go by our house so we would know they were in the area. We happened to be roofing our house and saw them as they came down the next road.

We have some very nice pictures of them up the pole fixing the broken insulators; my digital camera certainly has come in handy. Why couldn't they have fixed the problems three years ago and not have to go to this extent. They certainly seem to spend enough time avoiding fixing the problems, instead of getting to the bottom of it and upgrading the system. It was pretty comical watching them drive miles out of their way to avoid going past our house.

As another year closes out, we are no closer to a resolution than we were in 1998. We have learned an awful lot, the frustrating part of it is that Consumer's Energy has the control over all of it and they do not seem disposed to provide the solutions. Hopefully the Attorney General and the people of the State of Michigan will have the resources to make Consumer's Energy upgrade their distribution lines.

Wisconsin, Canada and other states are watching what happens in Michigan. In this year we have met and talked to many people that have had or are having the same problem that we ran into.

According to papers I received listing people in the state of Michigan who have been paid money from Consumer's Energy over the years; there are eight farmers in our area, one of them just two miles from us who had electrical problems. The area forms a circle from Standish to east of us to West Branch. Consumer's Energy redid the service in to one farm to three phase when we were having trouble with motors burning up, and we borrowed a motor from them. They wanted to sell us the motor because they were switching services. We did not know they had been having problems and were paid money.

When Consumer's Energy makes a settlement they put a gag order on the people and they can't talk about any of the details. Then when another farm in the area has a problem they don't know that their neighbor had the same problem. That is how the utility companies manage to get away with having the same problems in the same area and don't have to correct the problem. Why can't a solution be found? Why do so many lives have to turn upside down because a company has more money and time than we do? We know that things like this can happen but not to you. This is a David and Goliath fight!

Chapter 22

We have to make a trip to Jackson to the corporate headquarters for the depositions of Steve Wallenwine. He is short, has red hair, smiles and makes you feel like he only wants to be your friend. We meet with Bill Hendricks as well. He is tall, never cracks a smile; very much a company man. Bill Hendricks was the man who came to our house in the first place on December 10, 1998. He led us to believe he had never seen anything like the problems on our farm.

Now today he testifies that he has been on farms where he had seen symptoms of cows hesitating to come into the milk parlor, cows lapping water, cows dancing, or jumping. More than 300 farms had complained of these symptoms, the same exact things we had told them were happening on our farm. He then told how he had gone to Michigan State University to classes on "stray voltage". He had been to Wisconsin for classes and had even taught classes on "stray voltage.

Mr. Hendricks than talked about going to Don David's farm, a farm about two miles west of Vic Mier's farm on M-55 when they called him saying they had a problem. He went out there and identified a problem. At our farm he could not find any problems, so he would not go any further. Yet our cows were experiencing the same types of symptoms he indicated were a problem.

He also talked about going out to Sheryl Krantz farm which was about one mile south of us. She had told him she was getting shocks off her milking equipment. They moved her primary neutral pole away from her barn and that solved the issue.

When our daughter told him she had gotten shocks off our equipment, he just ignored her. He admitted that when lights blink there is a problem, or when the voltage goes below the minimum or over the maximum limit there is a problem, but he never asked anyone that could test for power quality to come out to our farm and test.

A pattern seems to be forming here. If they can find a problem that can not be attributed to Consumer's Energy, they are willing to resolve the issue, but if it looks like they could be liable, then you are on your own.

Here is someone who admitted he had the knowledge to be able to help us. I was in shock and discussed with Mr. Hendricks because he apparently did not care what happened to us. Instead he remained a company man. Brian had told him one time, at least we were able to sleep at night, our consciences were clear.

Steve Wallenwine was the next one to testify. He went over the testing he had done on our farm. He testified that at one time his department was referred to as Power Quality Department, but some time around 1996 the name was changed to Ag Services.

It was in 1996 when Consumers Energy in the Spees Memo identified the risk they had with "stray voltage" issues on farms with livestock. That was when they decided to split neutral or mechanically disconnect the electrical wires from all livestock farms. James Schrandt became head of that department. It allows Consumers to come when you complain of having a problem and tell you they can't possible be causing you a problem; they aren't connected to you. That must be a standard line because they tell every farmer the same thing. From this time forward, all agriculture issues go through James Schrandt's office.

Wallenwine said he remembered our request to have our Primary Neutral pole moved, but it was denied as not being necessary. Yet, when the Primary Neutral was moved at Sheryl Krantz's, she no longer was getting shocks off her equipment. When Alpena Power moved Mike Timm primary neutral, his cows' health improved.

It seems such a simple thing to keep us in business, when it worked somewhere else. When he was asked if there had ever been readings on the secondary side that exceeded .2 volts AC with the power off, his answer was, "I believe so." When asked if there were readings on the secondary side, which exceeded .2

volts with the power off, did he believe that it was incumbent upon Consumers Energy to have done something about that in accordance with its own engineering manual? His answer was, "It could have been looked at."

When he was asked if we had requested to have change made to the electrical system on our farm, he said, "My understanding is that it was evaluated and determined that changes were not necessary, that everything was well within standards. So when asked "So therefore, there were no changes made; correct?" The answer was, "There were no changes made."

Once again, the question of the video that Brian had taken of our heifers stepping came up. When asked, "If the Bellville's testify that you made a comment that the reason the cows were dancing was because of flies, would you dispute that?" His answer, was NO. This has always been a bone of contention because there was some reason that those heifers were moving their feet and in January there are no flies.

This was the barn that they measured more voltage on the water fountains, where no electricity was hooked to the fountains. Consumers had to come up with a reason and got caught. It certainly seems like they had the knowledge to help us. They had helped other farmers, and knew that there were other farmers in our area who had problems and those problems had been fixed or the farmers had been paid by Consumers. Why had they refused to help us?

I'm scared to death; we have to go through giving depositions. I don't know how long it will take to answer their questions or how they will twist our information. I have heard some awful stories about some things Consumers Energy is believed to have done to other farmers.

One farmer was getting ready to sue Consumers Energy and, as they were working on their case, a crop duster airplane flew over his farm on a clear day circled and came back and dropped his load of insecticide over the farmer's feed pile. Later Consumers Energy claimed the farmer was feeding bad feed to his cattle and that was what was making his cows sick, so he was unable to proceed with his case.

Another incidence was when two neighbors sued Consumers Energy. They were in court for the trial one day, when

Consumer's Energy attorneys told the one couple that if they dropped out of the case no charges would be filed against their son.

Their son was their milk hauler. He had parked his truck at home the night before and heard a noise during the night but did not see any thing. The next morning he did not check his truck, but went to pickup his parents" milk since they were his first stop.

He got about one half mile from his parents' farm when the police stopped him and accused him of having water in the milk in his truck. It is against the law for water to be added to milk. They were going to file charges and he could spend time in prison.

Hence, the offer from Consumers Energy at 10:00 a.m. The tests on whether there was water in the milk did not come in until noon. Needless to say, the parents dropped out of the court case. The other couple won their case and Consumers Energy appealed it. It took several years, but the case went to the Supreme Court of Michigan. It was sent back for retrial, but it is believed to have been settled out of court and disappeared.

Another case was at Swartz Creek. When that case was in court, the Judge got so disgusted with Consumers Energy attorneys that he locked the court room doors. He sent someone to Jackson to corporate headquarters for all the records on this farm and would not allow any one out of the courtroom or to telephone any one until he got the records. After he received the records and heard the case, the farmer was awarded $ 6, 000,000.00.

After all the stress of the court case and with Consumers Energy, the farmer died shortly after it was all over with at the age of 52. This is what we have to look forward to.

CHAPTER 23

Our depositions were at our attorney David Aldrich's office in Lansing a couple of weeks after the Jackson depositions. Mr. Michael Reynolds is the attorney for Consumers Energy. He comes into the room pulling boxes and boxes of material with him. He is short and round in stature, and gives the impression that he does not know what he is doing. But looks are deceptive, he is a bulldog.

Once when we had been to one of the court hearings last summer, he had acted friendly, asking about the information we had given our attorney. I had told him that we had taken twenty boxes to our attorney. When it was time to go before the Judge, he used that information against us. He said he had just learned that there was a bunch of information he had not received and he needed more time to prepare. After that I did not talk to him. He was no friend and I did not underestimate him, regardless of the way he appeared. Remember the story of "Little Red Riding Hood." He is the wolf.

The first thing I notice is that he is wearing a tie with cows on it. It also has streaks of yellow lines that look like lighting bolts. His comment is that his tie represents what happens to cows that come into contact with "stray voltage". It is a good thing I have a sense of humor, because instead being intimidated by him, I thought it was pretty comical.

Now it was my turn to compete with him and see who was going to win. Hopefully I will not make any mistakes. There is a lot of pressure on me. Our whole future may rely on my answers.

We start out explaining each picture that I took over the last few years. Mr. Reynolds the Consumers attorney, was interested in the group from the visit in December of 1999 when Consumers Energy came and looked at all the places I had told Mr. Schrandt about: The broken down grounds, the mini substation on Black road, the place where the grounded lines end coming from the school instead of continuing on to the substation like they are suppose to do. You could see the tracks in the snow. I think he was surprised that we knew that Consumers had been in the area. Whenever a Consumers truck was in the area, we would receive a phone call from someone and they would let us know there was activity.

We looked at pictures of cows that were thin; it was really hard to look at them again. These were animals that we had raised from babies and it hurt to see them in that condition and know there wasn't anything we could do for them. We looked at pictures of the Consumers workmen climbing the poles to repair the lines.

Then we got into my website. I have had a website since the year 2000. He wanted to know who was involved in SAFE. I told him I would like to make it a non-profit organization. This organization seems to bother them, but I don't intend to involve any one else in this until we get through this ordeal.

I had to explain pictures of our dog and of Kay, our daughter, riding her cow. We had to explain the pictures of the testing equipment mounted on the milking parlor floor.

Then we covered the testing that Don Hillman, the Attorney General, and Dave Stetzer had done on our farm. Then I had to defend the procedure we used to prepare our cows for milking. It was a good thing we had taken classes from Michigan Milk Producers, the company who purchased our milk. We were certified to have passed our classes.

We covered our veterinarians, who had come to our farm, and what they had told us. We went through all the things that had happened with our cows.

All of a sudden, Mr. Reynolds asked about a bill from fixing our computer feeder (this bin feeds the cows by a magnet on a chain around their neck). It was marked as an electrical problem. Having not seen this bill since 1995, I did not know what to say.

This guy liked to jump around and then hit you with some sharp point, so you had to stay on your toes. They had wanted all of our records, so we gave them all back to 1966, about twenty-nine crates worth. Mr. Reynolds said there was the October 1966 folder missing.

One of the things Mr. Reynolds hit us with was an evaluation form that Brian had filled out in 1994 at a meeting the MSU Cooperative Extension had put on in conjunction with Consumers Energy. Consumers Energy had paid for lunch. Consumers apparently had information at this meeting on "stray voltage".

Brian could not remember going to a meeting where Consumers presented any material and all the material I had kept over the years from seminars did not contain any such information. Consumers had offered to check farms at no charge to the farmer, so everyone at that meeting had taken advantage of the offer. Brian remembered that they had come to the farm and tested for "stray voltage", and had run a new wire.

I did not remember going to the meeting at all. I did remember that there had been a meeting that the weather had been really cold and I had stayed home to help keep the alley scraper going in the barn, and it took us all day. It is really hard to remember things that happen that many years ago.

I have learned there was a reason that Consumer's had those meetings. It gave them a date to start with the statute of limitations, kind of sneaky, but it did not surprise me. But they tested in 1994 and could not find a problem; I don't think we had a problem develop until later. As Mr. Aldrich, our attorney says, it is an on going situation that never ends.

We still have more questions to answer. We finally get to the "Magic Dust". I have been waiting for this question to come up. I knew that Mr. Reynolds would try to make us look stupid, but when we used the chicken grit we got relief. When we used, it the effects of the electricity would go away. In that January, we had cows coming in the milking parlor without having to drive them in to milk. We had more cows become pregnant. We had the highest milk production we had achieved in a long time.

I had really worried about how I was going to explain this without appearing to be totally crazy. One day we had been sitting in Mr. Aldrich's office and he gave me a book he had just purchased. When I opened it, it fell to a page about a method called salting. By salting you could change the resistance of the earth. It was a little creepy that I should find that page without reading the whole book, but I have said before God plays a big part in our story.

I do believe he opened the book to that page. When asked the question about the relief, I said, "There's a book, Power Quality Primer by Barry Kennedy. On page 164, you'll find a method that they called "salting." This is what we did when we spread the "chicken grit" around the primary neutral pole and the water well head."

I had made a history of what had happened with the cows. I don't know if that was good or bad. It helped me remember, but Mr. Reynolds used it to try to get us to stray from the facts. So we had a lot of "let the record stand."

It did help to outline the events. That was why I had done the history in the first place to know what date something happened instead of counting on memory.

We also used a calendar. So many things had gone on that we could not count on remembering every detail we had to go through when we had built our heifer barn. It was like an interrogation. We had not done anything wrong, but that is not the way Reynolds made us feel. We had to weigh each answer to try and guess if they could construe it the wrong way. It got a little trying and that was only the morning of the first day.

We ordered lunch in from a sandwich shop down the street. I was really upset. I did not want to eat with the Consumers Energy attorney!

During lunch the conversation was carried on by the two attorneys, I was having a hard time being social with Mr. Reynolds. Our attorney said "If you break bread with the other side, it's harder for them to be impersonal." I was really uncomfortable. Afterwards we went back to the interrogation. Who watched for cows in heat? How slippery were the floors in the barn? Who measured the voltage on the bolt in the wooden manager? How much milk were the cows giving? When were we first aware of the bovine leucosis in our herd?

We reported what we saw when the down ground was disconnected, the cows came into the milking on their own, did not kick the milkers off and what we saw when it was reconnected within twelve hours the cows would not come into the parlor on their own, kicked the milkers off again.

Did anyone else remark on the behavior change in our cows? I said yes, that our DHIA tester noticed the cows came in on their own and it did not take us as long to milk. He would come once a month and take milk samples to test for butterfat and weigh the amount of milk each cow gave. I learned that each time the Consumer's attorney Mr. Reynolds got an answer he did not like, we moved to another line of questioning. Then we hit a real snag. Mr. Reynolds wanted to know if any veterinarian had told us that the problems with our cows were due to electricity. I answered that they all said they did not have the knowledge on electricity to make that conclusion. It was one of the first times our attorney Dave Aldrich would have anything to say. It went like this:

Question: Okay, and to date no veterinarian has come forward and said, yes, this is the problem? Your livestock have been afflicted by stray voltage or some other type of electricity, fair to say?

Answer: None of the veterinarians I have dealt with have been knowledgeable enough to make a conclusion.

Question: Okay and none have?

Our attorney Mr. Aldrich: Well, that calls for speculation. I don't know if she knows that.

Question: None have voiced any conclusions to you?

Answer: Well, I wouldn't say that.

Question: Voiced any conclusions that your livestock were afflicted by stray voltage, fair to say?

Our attorney Mr. Aldrich: Well. I'm not sure she said that either. But go ahead. Maybe somebody did give you that opinion. So answer. That's fine.

Mrs. Belleville: We had a variety of discussions. And what their opinion might be with their knowledge in that field, they are not knowledgeable enough to make a recommendation, I guess, as to what ought to be done. Do they believe that they were afflicted, that they were being affected? They might believe that. You would have to ask them.

Question: What I'm asking you at this moment is, has any veterinarian told you that she or he believed that your livestock were being afflicted by stray voltage or any other type of electricity?

Answer: The veterinarians came to our farm and said that we had a problem. They all agreed with that.

Question: Okay. And what I want to find out is whether—and I'm just trying to get some discovery here—

Answer: Well, I think you've gotten everything from every veterinarian that we have talked to, unless you want to depose them. And if you want to depose them, then you can ask them that question.

Question: Well, what I'm asking you is whether or not any of them voiced to you an opinion that this problem that they told you about was by stray voltage or any other type of electricity?

Answer: Well, I guess I could tell you that Dr. Bartlett, and I told you previously, said that she had seen another calf that the legs fell off on another farm that had electrical problems. Dr. Dombrowski has talked to us.

Question: Okay, and what does Dr. Dombrowski say?

Answer: Well, he also did the herd health work on Vic Mier's farm and saw similarities between the two farms.

Answer (By Mr. Bellville); and also on Kartes.

Answer (By Mrs. Bellville): Right. He did work on Kartes' farm.

Question: Did Dr. Dombrowski tell you that he believed that the problems on your farm were caused by stray voltage or any other type of electricity?

Answer (By Mrs. Bellville): He said the similarities between the farms were—

Answer (By Mrs. Bellville): Very Similar.

Question: The question I'm asking is, and I will ask it until I get an answer, so we may be here for a—

(Our attorney) Mr. Aldrich: Well, it's an answer that you apparently want. She has given you an answer.

(Consumers attorney) Mr. Reynolds: It's a simple question and it really could be answered yes or no.

Mr. Aldrich: Well, it could be answered I don't know or I don't remember. There are more than two answers to that question.

Mr. Reynolds: That's correct.

Question: But what I want to know is whether or not at this point in time either Mr. or Mrs. Bellville recall any veterinarian believed that any of their problems with their herd were caused by stray voltage or any other type of electricity?

Answer (By Mr. Bellville): They're not trained in that field, so they just—

Answer (By Mrs. Bellville): I guess I would have to say if that's the kind of answer that you're looking for—

Question: Right.

Answer: Then I'm going to have to say I don't know because they are not trained in that field.

Question: Okay. The question I'm asking you though is, I mean, either you know that you recall or you do not know that you recall. But the question I'm asking you is: Do you recall one or more veterinarians telling you that she or he believed that your livestock had been adversely affected by stray voltage or any other type of electricity?

(Our attorney) Mr. Aldrich: I think she answered.

Mr. Bellville: I guess I have to say they are not trained in that and they have seen a similarity and that's all they say.

See what I mean about being interrogated? We had gone on and on about this point. To say any veterinarian had come on our farm, set up testing equipment and measured voltage levels would not have been correct. But they did say that our cows acted like cows on other farms where electrical influences had been present. Our cows exhibited almost all of the symptoms that Consumers outlined in their literature.

Of course it is not considered scientific by Consumers for a farmer to know how his cows are acting or when they are acting out of character. It is really trying to keep on your toes and not make any mistakes. Only one time did our attorney pull us out into the hall to talk to us.

We had been discussing our heifer barn; I had mentioned that we had trouble seeing our heifers in heat. Our attorney Dave Aldrich stopped the questions and took us into the hall. He wanted us to be careful what information we gave them and not admit we were having trouble with getting our heifers bred.

But I had then been going to say that we had always had no trouble getting them bred when we used the outside lot at our old barn. Then when we moved them inside with no outside lot we had some problems. As a result we built the outside lot the next spring. So we knew it was necessary to have outside lots.

This outside lot business had always upset me. All of these people who had talked to us in the last two years had known we had outside lots, now Consumers seem to be looking for an excuse for our cows not getting bred besides the electricity causing any problems.

We now have to defend all of our management practices, so when we went back into the depositions I had to make sure it was brought up, the fact that yes we had outside lots for all of our animals.

After that episode, our attorney, Dave Aldrich, relaxed and did not say any more for the rest of our deposition. So we must have been okay. Being put under a microscope and having every aspect of my life dissected was very emotional for me.

We finally moved on to another area of questioning. We talked about the feed we fed the cows. We talked about the cows falling down in the milking parlor. We had to go over our free stalls (where the cows laid down in between milking and at night). We talked about taking steel off the barn to let more air into the barn.

They had gone through all of our bills and knew that we had subscribed to Hoard's Dairyman magazine.

> Question: Okay. Hoard's Dairyman that was a publication to which you subscribed, right?

> Answer: off and on.

> Question: (By Mr. Reynolds) Is that what, I guess for want of a better term, would be referred to as the Bible of the dairy farmer?

> Answer: Not mine.

> Question: Do you recall any particular period of time when you did not subscribe to Hoard's Dairyman?

> Answer: There was a significant period of time when we did not subscribe to it.

> Question: How come?

> Answer: I didn't send subscriptions back. And when you get thirty magazines and you get a substantial number you don't have to pay for, why pay for one? We were always so busy we never had time to read all the magazines that came free or not.

Then he asked us if we watched 60 Minutes. I told him the same thing. It came on at chore time and we were busy.

> Question: Did you ever hear other farmers talking about watching the 60 Minutes show on stray voltage?

> Answer: (By Mrs. Bellville) I didn't even know there had been a program.

> Question: Okay. Where was it that you picked up these passing references about stray voltage before January 25, 1998?

Answer: To tell you the truth, I'm not sure. I mean, we all know what heart attack is. That's the kind of passing knowledge.

Question: So you had heard?

Answer: I had heard the word.

Question: And you associated it with negative impacts on cows?

Mr. Aldrich, our attorney: Well, she hasn't said that at all.

Mrs. Bellville: No. No, I had heard the word. I asked you for a definition because I don't really know what the definition is.

Question: The question, and I'm only—you said you had heard these passing references to it and I just wanted to know the references you had heard. Were they in any way associated with dairy livestock?

Answer, Mrs. Bellville: I don't even know at this point in time. I can't tell you when I might have heard it. It's like heart attack. It's like diabetes. Those are words. But do you look them up to know what they mean? No. So at this point I can say I don't know.

We finally got into whether Consumer's Energy had ever intentionally told us any thing that was false. My answer was yes, we were told we had quality power, and when you drop it below 114 volts-162 times, that's not quality power.

Question: When were you told that you had quality power?

Answer: Mr. Schrandt and I had a discussion about the 162 times.

Question: You told him that this was recorded, is that right?

Answer: Yes.

Question: And he told you that notwithstanding that he felt that you had quality power?

Answer: Yes.

Question: Did you believe him?

Answer: No. Not when it drops below the limit 162 times. That's with their equipment.

Mr. Aldrich, our attorney: Can we have a date at this point in time, because your belief in them may have changed over time.

Mrs. Bellville: Well, it certainly did. After they were there in February of 1999 and this stuff started happening—the vacuum pump was in June of 2000—my belief in them had certainly dwindled.

Question: Okay. When was it that they told you that you weren't having problems, even if the vacuum pump was turning off?

Answer: (By Mrs. Bellville) They would walk on our farm today and tell me I didn't have a problem.

Finally after about nine hours of interrogation we were finished. But we are not done. Mr. Reynolds still wants to ask more questions, so we set another date. Brian and I went down to our attorney's office and I burst into tears. I had been terrified all day of saying the wrong thing, but I think I held my own. Brian does not have a good memory for detail so I had to answer most of the questions. It is like playing a chess game. They are not going to get the best of me or win.

Dave Aldrich said I had done a good job. When you tell the truth, it is not all that hard to remember, but Mr. Reynolds sure likes to twist the things you say. I'm beginning to figure out their tactics and the game they play. They try to make you second guess yourself, doubt yourself, and blame yourself. Thank God, that much is over. After spending the day across the table from Consumers Energy attorney I felt I could just about take anything any one wanted to send our way. I'm exhausted!

Chapter 24

Several things bothered me about that day; the first was the Seminar evaluation sheet that Brian had signed. We checked with the MSU County Extension agent, to see if he could remember anything about that day. He said that it had been a really cold day and the attendance had not been really good in the morning.

People kept straggling in. They had equipment that didn't run, drinkers frozen; it took longer to do chores, so people ran behind. He did not think Brian got there until noon.

We checked with the water treatment plant. They keep records on the temperature. In January of 1994, the weather had been 23 degrees below zero for three days. I could remember a time when we had a stretch of cold weather for that long. We had to get up in the middle of the night to run the alley scraper (these were scrapers that came down each alley in the barn, to keep the alleys clean where the cows stayed). When the floors got cold, we had trouble because the waste did not flow. It got stiff and we had to use a wheel barrow to haul it down the alley to the gutter. So I had to stay home from that meeting to help with the alleys. Consumer's Energy apparently is going to use this signed paper against us to prove we had been told about "stray voltage".

Apparently about that time Consumer's Energy spent a lot of time going across the state to meetings, sending the video, and literature to try to start a statue of limitations date.

The other thing that bothered me was the bill that had a notation on it about a power surge. Consumers wanted to claim that we had electrical problems before we thought we did. I looked at our bookkeeping records, and the check we got for the payment from the insurance company on the computer feeder was entered as lightning damage. That should take care of that one.

When we had to turn over all of our bills, pictures, files—everything, felt we did not have an identity. I had been used to looking up something if we had a question about it. We had kept every bill and all the information from all the meetings we had attended since 1966 after we were married. Now our life was in the attorney's office in Lansing. It is really a strange feeling, being at loose ends.

Our lives have taken such a turn. We just wanted to milk our cows, raise our family and farm until we wanted to retire. Life has such twists and turns, we never know what is in store for us. The most frightening part of all of this is not being able to plan our next move. We never know what the future will bring, but once upon a time we had goals and future plans. Now our life is in limbo.

CHAPTER 25

We are back in Lansing for our second day of depositions. I feel more confident. We wait for Mr. Reynolds to haul his boxes of material into the room. He has a cold so he is not feeling really well, poor man. He is also minus the cow tie. We're back to the seminar that Brian attended in West Branch.

Question: Do you recognize a receipt for attending a seminar entitled "Managing the Dairy Cow's Environment for Greater Profitability?"

Answer: That's what it looks like.

We then go to the article that was in the Ogemaw dated April 13, 2000.

Question: And do you recall reading this portion here where Mr. MacInnis talks about your attendance or your husband's attendance at the January 19,1994 seminar entitled Managing the Dairy Cow's Environment for Greater Profitability?

Answer: Mr. MacInnis states that.

Question: Okay. And going to Exhibit No. 163, is this a letter that you wrote to the Ogemaw County Herald in response to that particular article?

I had written several articles to the papers that summer in answer to the articles that Consumers had put in. If they were not worried about us they would have just ignored us, but it caused quite a stir, the community was asking questions of Consumers.

Answer: It appears to be.

Question: And in that particular letter, did you in fact indicate that you had in fact attended that seminar at Michigan State in 1994.

Mr. Aldrich: Which paragraph?

Question: Paragraph number seven, I believe.

Answer: (By Mrs. Bellville) I didn't specifically say we attended that seminar. I said we have attended many of the MSU seminars over the years.

Question: And you said, as Mr. MacInnis indicates, we attended a MSU seminar in 1994, is that correct?

Answer: I said—

Mr. Aldrich: Well, it speaks for itself.

Mr. Reynolds: I'm just asking her if she wrote that.

Mrs. Bellville: I said, as Mr. MacInnis indicates, we attended an MSU seminar in 1994. So he does know we work closely with the college. In fact, Cooperative Extension was the first people we contacted.

As I said before, when Mr. Reynolds does not get an answer he wants, he switches to another topic. We went back to the Hoards Dairyman publication.

Question: Did you read an article called, "Third of Farms Tested Had Cow Area Stray Voltage", "There Are Causes to Problems Other Than Stray Voltage", "Electrical Service Hasn't Kept Up With Dairy Farm Needs", A Dairyman's Response to the Stray Voltage Article", "Stray Voltage Handbook Available from USDA", "Wisconsin's Electrical Code Helps Fight Stray Voltage", or "Experts Are Split on Equal potential Planes."

My answer to all of the articles was that I did not remember reading any of them, so we went back to it.

Question: Can you recall ever reading any Hoard's Dairyman article on stray voltage or any other effects of electricity on livestock?

Answer: No. I read the Reader's Digest every month and I can't tell you what I read in Reader's Digest. That's the only magazine I did read because I liked it.

We seem to spend a lot of time going over the same territory. We than moved to another topic. We're back to the visit by Bill Hendricks on December of 1998. Hendricks had told us that the problem was all farmers who had problems in the area, all used the same bulls on our cows, when I had said the only thing we all had in common was electricity. At the time we had believed him. Electricity might not be the cause of our problems.

When asked the question: At that point in time, did you believe what he said?

Answer: At that point in time I had no reason to disbelieve what he said, although since then I have discovered how much knowledge he had when he walked on the farm that we did not have.

Question: What knowledge was that?

Answer: He had already been to "neutral to earth voltage school." He had already read Understanding Neutral to Earth Voltage, the book. He had tested over 300 farms. According to the advertisements, he had been over 7,000 farms. He had an extremely large amount of knowledge on the subject which we did not possess.

Then we skipped to questions about the Agrivolt system. Mr. Reynolds wanted to know what Agrivolt found out when they tested our house, whether they indicated or not that there were problems coming onto our farm from Consumers, from the utility. Agrivolt advised us there were problems coming from the utility and if we purchased their equipment for $30,000.00, it would solve our problems. At this time Consumers was to come and test, so we waited for them. There were a couple of farms in the area who had purchased the Agrivolt system and we wanted to see if it helped them.

Also we were still trying to find out if that was our problem or not. That was just too much money to invest if it was not going to work.

We went back over the testing done by Consumers; how we had asked them to go down to our heifer barn and test, and they refused to go there. Then we moved to questions about why we had not gone to using a bull to breed our heifers and cows. This was something I felt very strongly about. We had always, with one exception, bred our animals by using artificial insemination. For me it was a safety issue. There have been many farmers injured or killed when bulls attack them. We had a young daughter and hired people who we needed to be concerned about. I was so adamant about this that there was a salesman I backed against a door one day and told him if he wanted to come back, bulls were not a subject we were going to pursue.

We covered some of the interrogatory answers we had given; seems like we have covered this material before and he just wants us to give a different answer. I will say Mr. Reynolds certainly is a bulldog. All morning we have been going over material on Mr. Schrandt's visit to our house. This was arranged by Farm Bureau to try to keep things out of the court system, but Consumers would not fix anything or admit that there were any problems so we had no choice but to sue them.

We ordered lunch again, and it was a little easier to sit with Mr. Reynolds and eat. Lunch actually got quite funny. We had sandwiches, chips and a big pickle. Mike Reynolds did not like pickles and he went into a litany on how much he disliked pickles. Mr. Aldrich ate his pickle and we all laughed about it.

One time during our depositions Mr. Reynolds said, he should get Consumers to hire me after our court case was done because he had never seen anyone so organized who knew so much about electricity. I'm not sure if that remark was to make me feel impressed and let my guard down. I just laughed. We proceeded to go back to the questions.

Now he wants to know how I met Cecil Angell, a reporter from the Detroit Free Press. Cecil had called us and wanted to write an article about our farm as well as Vic and Rose Meir's. Mr. Reynolds wanted to know if the articles were correct. I said that some of the articles that had been written had some incorrect information in them. He wanted to know if we had corrected them. With all of the articles, we never had the opportunity to proof read them and were not given the chance to correct misquotes. He then moved to the articles in the Bay City Times. I had to point out to him that some of these articles confused our farm with Vic Mier's. We never had the opportunity to see the articles before they were printed.

We're back to a bill from July 31, 1995 for $4000.00. Had we been told or had heard that a high voltage surge may have damaged our computer feeder, milking system and automatic detacher? It has been a long time and we don't remember what the problem was that occurred. It really is hard to remember every thing that happened. That is why we keep records to revert back to, but they have all of our records, so I have no idea what happened.

Now we're on to a copy of a return receipt requested dated June 27, 1995. It has my signature on it.

> Question: Do you recall getting this pamphlet along with the return receipt entitled "It takes a lot of Energy to Run a Farm?"
>
> Answer: No, possibly because that's haying time. We have very little time to read much of anything.

Like most farmers, we just never really knew or suspected we had a problem with "stray voltage". If we would ever have thought we had any problem with electricity, we would not have waited until 1999 to investigate. How dumb does he think we are to run a business and let a problem run for a number of years without questioning anything? If we'd have had an indication of any problems back then, I can assure you I would have moved heaven and earth to come up with a solution. It really irritates me that they choose to believe we would ignore a problem with our cattle for that many years without trying to find a solution. We did not have any suggestion of a problem until the fall of 1998, and then we did try to find out what the problem was and to find a solution to it. The road block was Consumers Energy! Now we have to sit here and answer all of these questions. We have to defend all of our actions since 1966. What we read, who we talked too, what we said.

We're back to the inclusion of Diane Talicksa's animals into our herd. Consumers Energy would like to blame everything on these cows. She had approached us to house her animals. She had them on another farm and wasn't happy with where they were at. This herd of animals' body score was about 1.5, very thin, when they came to our farm in November of 1995. When they left in January, 1997, they scored 3.0. We had treated her cows just like they were ours. We had vaccinated all the animals the same. At that time we were not having problems; that developed a year and half later.

If any illnesses would have been present from her herd, it would not have taken one and a half years to develop.

We moved into the fact that in 1989 we had our hutches located in a space between our silos and the road, which happened to be under the electrical distribution lines. We had a problem in 1989. The day after Thanksgiving, we started losing calves. They would be okay when they were fed in the morning and be dead by night. We started feeding them three times a day. That did not help. We took a couple down to MSU to be tested and they could not find any reason for them to die. We had the veterinarians there almost everyday and they could not come up with a reason. They did not have pneumonia or anything that might be a normal problem. It got so bad that our daughter who was feeding them, cried and refused to feed them thinking it was her fault. We lost forty calves during this time and they stopped dying as soon as it got cold and the ground froze.

When Consumers Energy came out one of the times and did some measurements, they measured ninety volts bleeding off the distribution lines and when they measured where we had moved the calves after we built our last barn, it measured five volts. We had noticed that we had lost fewer calves when we moved the pens to their present location, but no one ever mentioned that the electricity could cause them a problem. As we had found out, Thanksgiving was our worst time of the year. We also know that the ground resistance makes a difference and, when the ground freezes, it is not as good a conductor for the electricity. All of these things Consumers is aware of but the average person is not.

Now we go to the video of the heifers stepping in the barn down the road. Did we do any electrical testing that day? (Unlike the testing done by Dave Stetzer, there were voltage measurements superimposed on the bottom of the screen.) This video only shows the heifers moving their feet. It doesn't collate any electrical measurements to show the amount of voltage in the ground to cause the heifers to step around.

Then we had to cover several letters that were written to us or that we had written to someone else. We had written a letter to Ernie Birchmier from Michigan Farm Bureau in January of 2000. I had hoped that Farm Bureau could help us. Another question covered Dr. Sanders' letter whether we had given permission for him to have access to the test results or not. The answer was no. I know that in his letter he mentioned the testing, and I know he had gotten a couple of pages, but not the entire report. Then we got into my testifying for the Michigan Attorney General in her suit against Consumers Energy. Attorney General Frank Kelley had started the suit five years before after receiving over 700 complaints from farmers. When Jennifer Granholm became Attorney General, she decided to pursue the case. He wanted to know if it was still correct. I said yes. As I have said before, the truth is the truth.

We went over the fact that the tests by Larry Wallman in June of 2000, which had been arranged by the Attorney General's office but not part of her case against Consumers Energy, seeing the voltage went as low as 106.9. And Consumers said he did not have the equipment set up correctly. Consumers decided to do their own testing with their own equipment and the voltage went as low as 107. Consumers would not admit that there was a problem then when they could not dispute the test.

We then moved to our health book that we kept on all of the calves that were born. I explained the terms DOA—dead on arrival, laid on calf (for some reason the cow lay on the calf and it was dead), Dutch-belted, a particular breed of animal that were mostly black in color and had a white belt behind their front legs around their body. We moved to the sheet where I had kept the number of cows sleeping in the free stalls where the cows laid between milkings. Then we moved into the sheets where we kept track of cows given antibiotics and when their milk was okay to go back into the milk tank. At this time it was 4:45 p.m. in the afternoon and we were finally done for the day. It was such a relief to be done, but only for today. We must come back again!

Someone had given us a film to watch. The farm family in the film was having problems with "stray voltage." The son and his wife come home to the farm because Mom and Dad are having problems with their cows. The film shows the veterinarians coming out to the farm and shaking their heads over the cows dying. They can't come up with a reason. The cows are in a stanchion barn. The son comes out to the barn and four or five cows are laying there dead. The farmer and son decide that the problem is electricity coming into the barn and they contact the utility company. The company won't repair the lines. In one scene, the daughter-in-law goes into the kitchen and turns on every electrical appliance before sliding down the cabinets to the floor sobbing. This is where the husband finds her. I cried. This was too realistic; whoever wrote this movie had gone through this electricity issue. The son goes out and rips the electric lines down that come into the farm. It ends with the neighbors helping them build new electric lines to the farm to solve the problem.

That is what needs to be done at our farm, and if you could solve it that easy, it would really be nice! There is a farm in our area that wants to build a new milking parlor. Consumers Energy finally told them that they would build a grounded wire, the best electricity the utility could give them, for two and a half miles, so that they would not have "stray voltage". It cost the farmer $40,000, a small price to pay for no dead cows or burned up equipment. We offered to pay for new wire to our farm, but Consumers Energy would not do that for us.

CHAPTER 26

Another week and we're back down at Lansing for hopefully our last day of depositions. Now I guess I could say I'm angry. The first day I was scared; the second day we got through; today is battle day. I think I'm learning where Consumers is going with their questions and it doesn't take long to prove me right.

Question: Going back to the seminar in West Branch, do you remember when you received a fluke 70 meter?

Answer: No.

We're back to pamphlets and do we remember them. As before we told Reynolds, we have not found any Consumers literature that we would have received before 1998. I now have a lot of Consumers information. I have not found any of it from before1998 and I have gone through every seminar we have attended over the years dating back to our first seminar after we were married. If we would have received this material, it would have been there.

During our depositions, Mr. Reynolds played the video that Consumers had sent out to dairy farmers in 1994. I had been so upset with it. The film pointed out the things to look for if a "stray voltage" problem existed. Most of the things outlined in the film were happening on our farm. If we would have seen that film, we would have known what was going on instead of spending all that time trying to come up with an answer.

Question, Mr. Reynolds: Back in early 1994, were you observing any avoidance of areas or equipment by any of your dairy livestock?

Answer: According to that film, when my daughter got shocks off the milking equipment, they ignored her. That's hard to take. One of the first things that the film said was, if you or any of your employees are getting shocks off your equipment that was from "stray voltage". Do you think I would have let my daughter get shocked for years?

That makes me angry! We go back over the video that Dave Stetzer, the electrician from Wisconsin, had taken when he was at our farm in 2000. Then we go to the video of our sale of the cows and how some cows were removed to not be sold.

Question: Was there any reason why you wouldn't perhaps put them out there, see if somebody might be interested in buying them for more than you could get if you just took them to be beefed?

Answer: No. There is no auction sale that I know of when you sell your herd of cows that you don't remove the cows that are questionable. You're selling the best of the animals that you can.

We go back to a letter written by Monty Reichard from Purina. He had made some reference to cow comfort issues. We said that we had replaced some of the free stalls after that letter, and it did not make any difference in how many cows slept in the stalls. Then we moved to the video done by Channel 5; why they had come up to our house. They came up for the meeting in March, 2000, at Logan Township hall. We went back to the letter from Monty Reichard. Did we have any discussion with Mr. Reichard about feeding heifers like feed-lot steers which are pushed to gain weight?

Answer by Mrs. Bellville: I'm not sure we had a discussion with him. He was balancing the ration at that point in time. We had switched to feeding more grain in the winter because of the fact that it's colder weather, and we had probably gone off it towards spring or would have. So this was in February. So they could have been on a higher corn diet at that point in time. They do have an exercise lot. So I'm not sure what he is talking about there. He is aware there was an exercise lot they were using.

Like some of the others, I think he has a lot of clients and may get them mixed up on occasion.

Question: There were some people who expressed to you that they thought you had an acidosis problem, weren't there, such as Dr. Erskin or Dr. Sanders?

Answer: Dr. Sanders never mentioned it. Dr. Erskin came up and did stomach PHs as one of the things–like we did bovine— the BVD testing. We also pulled samples of PH on cows for acidosis testing. None of those levels were outside of the normal range. So when he came, we looked over different things that there could be a problem with. At no time did he find a problem with acidosis.

Question: As a result of your meeting, did you form any opinions as to whether or not Dr. Sanders would give you a fair appraisal of what was going on or a biased one?

Answer: For $1.6 million, I'm not sure you can be unbiased.

Question: I guess that's something that obviously someone would have to decide besides you and me. But I'm just asking what your impressions were as a result of talking with him for those three to four hours.

Answer by Mrs. Bellville: I thought it was a waste of time basically. He did not go over anything other than suggesting that we have a team from MSU come up. There was no electrical testing. There was no looking at forages. There was no walking through the barn, looking at the cows to see they were laying in the stalls or what condition they were in. We stood in our office and basically chit-chatted for two and half hours over rations that were not new rations. They were not rations that we were feeding at that particular time. I felt actually that North Star had done a better job looking at the ration and looking at the feed lengths than Dr. Sanders did.

Question: When you received Dr. Sanders' letter of October 12th, 1999, did you have any concerns when you saw him write "the herd is being fed a ration which is causing rumen acidosis?

Answer: Yes. Because I would like to know how he determined that when the rations he had looked at, were not current rations and had been told so. And he did not look at the feed that we were feeding that particular day. Nor had he done any stomach PHs. It's very difficult to make that kind of a diagnosis without going to anything further to back that up. And we had already done that. Michigan State had done testing and could not find any acidosis.

Question: Were you using needles to inject a number of cows prior to June of 1999?

Answer: We did not use individual needles until we discovered we had bovine leukemia. And then the recommendation was to use single needles. Also the vets do not use single needles on farms. None of us were ever told to use single needles until we discovered we had bovine leukemia. And that was the recommendation that I was given. It was not a recommendation by the vets. And the vets to this day still use one needle on multiple injections such as Bangs vaccinations. They may use a separate needle per farm. They do not use a separate needle per individual. So now you're looking at a recommendation that was given to us that the veterinary practices don't even use.

Question: Well, did you have laminitis at that at that time?

Answer: There were some cows that may have had laminitis. We also notice that there are different times of the year that cows are lame more than they are at others times. If you want to correlate that with anything, when there's high usage, high electrical usage, the cows will limp more. If you get cool weather, they won't. If you get a stretch of hot weather where there's a lot of electricity used, a lot of air-conditioners. The cows will develop lameness within a couple days. And there is no feed switch at that point. So there are some observations that are being made that the total picture may not be looked at also. And we discussed that at a later point in time.

Question: With whom?

Answer: Dr. Erskin.

Question: And what did he say?

Answer: He had not dealt with a farm exactly like ours, nor observed some of the things that we were observing. It's one of those fine lines that whether they want to cross it or not. At one point in time we asked them to use our farm as a test farm and do research.

Question: On?

Answer: On electricity and the influences. And taking an infield farm rather than trying to do laboratory testing. You can't duplicate the same thing in a laboratory, and that's where all the testing has been done.

Question: And what was Dr. Erskin's response to your offer?

Answer: That would have to be made at a university level.

Question: And you never heard?

Answer: We sold the cows.

Question: If you could go to number thirty-three there. It's a letter from Mr. Durst to you dated, November 3, 1999. And at the bottom of the first page, under the section of nutrition, it says: "The most important area to focus attention on is nutrition and nutrition management. It appears that cows have suffered periodic acidosis. Therefore, it is important to one, feed rations that substantially reduce the risk of causing acidosis: and two, feed them in ways that as much as possible do not allow individual cows to have acidosis due to selectivity of feed." Now, did that cause you concerns that you had some acidosis problem after reading that in the letter?

Answer: No. Because I think its one thing that everybody wants to latch onto—, is to blame it on acidosis. And yet the PH levels showed there wasn't an acidosis problem. The other things they looked at showed there wasn't an acidosis problem. But if cows don't eat and don't drink, then they become selective eaters themselves. And if you look at the electrical part of the problem and part of the thing that it says is that they don't eat and don't drink—then they back away from feed. But is that a secondary rather than a primary? We balanced the rations. Everything was set into place. And do I think we had an acidosis problem? The PH levels never showed that. And that's the one indicator that they used. Otherwise it's very difficult to determine that.

Question: Were any rumen taps done on the cows after this November.

Answer: No. That was not one of their suggestions. And I guess my opinion is if they were very, very concerned about it being an acidosis problem, that should have been one of the first things that they set out to do. And that wasn't one of their suggestions. So therefore, they didn't seem to think it was a major problem or they would have addressed it doing stomach PHs. And they didn't.

Question: Did you discuss this letter with any or all of the people, either Mr. Durst or the people he was signing for?

Answer: We may have discussed parts of it that pertain to those particular individuals. Buchholz, Dill, Simkins, Helmrich, were all involved in the nutritional part of it. Dr. Risley was there as a veterinarian because he wanted to learn more about nutrition. How much of it we actually went over with any of them, I'm not really sure. We put into practice the things that they suggested. And we were due to have another meeting in April, which we did.

Question: Did you ever discuss acidosis with any of those people?

Answer: I don't think that it was brought up after that. I guess my concern is that if Dr. Risley or Dr. Erskin or any of the others, felt there was such a problem with acidosis they would have done a regimented PH rumen tap every two week. The vet was there every two weeks, and we could have pulled cows in every two weeks. Nobody seemed to want to do that to verify it. That was their suggested or what they wanted to pin it on, but nobody ever followed through to—and we cannot pull the PH. That has to be done by a veterinarian. And he didn't make that a regimen or make the recommendation to do so. So therefore, it leads me to believe that they didn't think it was a major problem.

Mr. Reynolds: That's the last question I have about that letter. So why don't we take a quick break here and enjoy the sandwiches.

Yes, we had to listen to the fact that he did not like pickles; once again Mr. Aldrich ate his pickle. This was our third lunch with the enemy; it has gotten a lot easier to handle. Mr. Reynolds is just a man doing his job. He failed to intimidate me, and I think I have held my own, but I sure will be glad when this is over.

After lunch we switched into our financial circumstances. We covered the 1980's when interest rates were 20%. We were covering our bills until 2000 when our veterinary bills reached $20,000. We had lost fifty-eight cows in 1999 and fewer than 100 cows were milking in 2000 when we should have been milking 140–160 cows without beginning to have a major impact. Expenses were more than normal and the income was less. We then went back to a list I had made of the twenty samples. I had broken down the years 1990, '91, '92, '93, '94, '95, and '96. Then I had marked them negative or positive.

This led to a question because ten cows were born before 1995, and three tested positive for bovine leucosis. And out of the ten cows that were born in 1995 and 1996, that seven were positive, is that right?

Answer: Correct.

Question: Were you making any effort at that point in time to try correlate whether or not the introduction of the livestock from Diane Taliksa's herd may have had any impact on the bovine leucosis in your herd?

Answer: No. That splitting mark designates when the tower went on line in September of 1994, and her cows did not come until November of 1995.

Question: Okay. Has anyone ever told you that any electrical phenomena emanating from that radio tower has caused bovine leucosis in your herd?

Answer: No. I only know what I have read in the book on one study that was done with microwaves and mice and that 30 percent of them had leukemia when they were killed.

Now we're going back to the pictures. That is where we started our deposition. We look at pictures of steers with crooked legs. Then we look at some of the pictures that were taken at various places that Consumers toured in December of 1999. Next we covered the pictures Brian took when the Public Service Commission came up with Consumers and did some testing at the substation. Then we looked at a picture of our youngest daughter sitting on her cow.

Question: Did you have any concerns when you saw or heard about this that your daughter was on the back of a cow?

Answer: Not if that's her pet cow. I mean, her pet cow is one she raised from a calf at the fair. She likes to ride horses. She decided, I guess, to ride the cow. My oldest daughter had taken a bunch of pictures around the farm and we had to go through those. One of them was the monitor that was in the barn office. It showed the voltage on Thanksgiving Day.

Question: What do you mean?

Answer: Well, the electrical usage on Thanksgiving Day is the worst day of the year for electrical usage.

Question: People watching the football games?

Answer: No. They start cooking turkey at 5:00 in the morning and they get done at 8:00 o'clock at night. And this was just showing that a lot of the times the pink line and the blue line were together. When the electricity gets really bad, they split farther apart and you get all this, a lot of spikes on it. So, that's why the picture was taken, to show that that's what the screen looked like on Thanksgiving.

Question: Have any of the people that purchased any of your livestock after or at the August 5th sale, complained to you at all about the health, production or reproduction of any of those cows or heifers or calves that they purchased from you?

Answer: No. The only couple of guys that have talked to us were well-satisfied with their animal. No one has ever called to complain about anything.

We went back to the visit we made to the Arlen Walts farm, where we met Dr. Grahman, and was asked if we had met Bill English, or if he had done any testing at our house, which he had not done. Had we ever talked to Alex Furo, an electrical engineer from Canada? He has a cottage on Sage Lake and comes over a couple of times a year. Had we ever discussed his work for the Minnesota Science Advisors Group?

Answer: The summary disposition on it was that it was all the farmer's fault and they were bad managers. And that was the part he objected to—his belief was that that was not what the study showed.

Question: Other than discussing his work with these, this Minnesota group, did you have any other discussions with Mr. Furo regarding stray voltage or any other form of electricity and its effect on livestock?

Answer: He had done some work in Canada at this particular farmer's farm also and the work that the Canadians are now doing to try and solve the problem in Canada, which they are now recognizing is a huge issue.

In the fall of 1999, a group of Canadians came over to meet with the Michigan Farm Bureau. A farmer, Lee Montgomery had fought with the utilities in Canada for many years; he had a herd that won several production awards. He sued the utility, and when they tore down the substation near him, his cows were better. His daughter wrote a story about when they bought goldfish, the fish would live at the daughter's home but they would die at Lee's house. Then we went back over material we had covered in the other two days of depositions. We talked about what happened when the primary neutral was disconnected. I had made a notation, and Mr. Reynolds wanted me to read it out loud.

Answer: "November 30, 1999, pole at Eldridge's, measures nine volts. Heifers not eating, some won't put heads in the metal headlocks. Heifers have gone down from 1800 pounds a feed twice a day to 800 pounds of feed, had to disconnect Elbridge's primary neutral. They started to eat again and we saw an increase in feed intake on the cows, also a milk increase until the cows developed dysentery. They were starting to come up when Consumers hooked up the neutral again."

We continue to go over more things we have already covered; Mr. Schrandt's visit, letters from Phil Durst.

Question: Other than yourselves, is there anyone else that you're aware of that could verify that there was a marked increased in the health, production, reproduction of your herd during the time period when the primary neutral down ground was disconnected?

Answer: The feed intake sheets show it. The milk increase shows it. It's marked on there when the dysentery starts. I told Phil Durst that the cows were coming into the milking parlor better.

Question: Anybody else that was out there during that time frame that observed or had the opportunity to observe the cows?

Answer: Duane Reinke. And during the time in January we were—it was a longer period of time and we had cows settled. And the comments at that time were raised because cows settled during that period of time. The cows came in the milking parlor that the tester observed. Milk production went up. Somatic cell count went down, and everyone questioned what had been done to make those things show up like that.

Question: Anyone else during the time period that this magic dust was put around other than Mr. Reinke?

Answer: Well, I told you the team from MSU questioned that period of time and what we had done to achieve those things that I mentioned.

At 6:40 P.M. the deposition were concluded and the witnesses excused. Thank goodness that is over! After three days, 631 pages of testimony, I think we did okay, but it gives us an idea what it will be like when we go to trial.

After we went back to Mr. Aldrich's office he handed me a report. It was affidavits from Dr. Timothy Eyth and Dr. Ronald Risley. They were almost identical.

I, Timothy Eyth, D.V.M., swear that the following information is based upon personal knowledge, and that I can and will testify to its truth if called as a witness in this case:

1. I am a doctor of veterinary medicine, I was first licensed to practice veterinary medicine in 1969, and I am currently licensed to practice veterinary medicine in the State of Michigan.

2. Recently, I retired from an active veterinary practice with West Branch Veterinary Services, located in West Branch, Michigan. A large percentage of my veterinary practice involved dairy livestock. During the course of my career as a veterinarian, I familiarized myself with some scientific literature regarding the effects of "stray voltage" and other electrical phenomena on dairy livestock.

3. For more than fifteen years, I served as a regular veterinarian for the dairy herd of Brian and Nancy Bellville, located on Nansue Dairy Farm in Prescott, Michigan. Other veterinarians at West Branch Veterinary Services also visited and treated the Bellville herd, both as part of a regular herd health program and as needed.

4. Over the course of the years, particularly in 1999–2000, I and others at West Branch Veterinary Services also consulted with a number of experts from and through Michigan State University and its Extension program to assist us in addressing problems with the Bellville dairy herd, including Drs. Erskine, Grooms, Mellenberger, Bucholtz and Sanders.

5. It is my understanding that the Bellville's have filled a "stray voltage" lawsuit against Consumers Energy, claiming that it was responsible for damaging their herd's health, milk production, and reproduction.

6. The Bellville's have provided me with reports from those who conducted electrical testing for "stray voltage" and other electrical phenomena on and near their farm, and have discussed them with me.

7. Based upon my own research into this issue, as well as my familiarity with the herd, its health, and its management, I have not seen any data that has convinced me that the Bellville dairy herd was afflicted by "stray voltage" or any other electrical phenomena.

8. Though the Bellville's complained about it to me, I never observed any unusual behavior by their dairy livestock, such as any unusual reluctance to enter the milking parlor, any unusual kicking off milkers, any unusual drinking or eating behavior, any reluctance or refusal to drink or eat, or any unusual lifting of feet.

9. I have never been electrically shocked on any of my visits to the Bellville farm, nor have I heard or seen anyone being shocked while I was there.

10. The Bellville herd did experience a number of adverse veterinary diseases or conditions (such as a tremendous number of displaced abomasums, lameness, milk fever, and ketosis), which we at West Branch Veterinary Services believed were caused by an improper or overly-changed nutrition regimen, and not "stray voltage" or any other phenomena.

11. We at West Branch Veterinary Services also believed that the Bellville herd was confronted by some comfort challenges, including a number of uncomfortable free stalls and an overly smooth floor in the free stall barn. Such conditions can adversely affect a dairy cow's health, production, and reproduction.

12. It is my opinion that any reproduction problems experienced in the Bellville herd are mainly attributable to poor heat detection by the Bellville's, and were not caused by "stray

voltage." Because the herd seldom was let out into the yard where it could easily be seen, the already difficult task of heat detection was made harder because the Bellville's were forced to rely upon secondary indications of heat and programmed breeding. Keeping the cows on cement most of the time also further reduced their ability to detect heat considerably. The Bellville's also adamantly refused our suggestion to breed their heifer and cows with a bull that could easily detect heat, and instead, continued to rely solely on artificial insemination.

13. It is my understanding that the Bellville's are alleging that "stray voltage" damaged the immune systems of their dairy livestock. I do not recall us doing any specific immune system testing. Except for some abscesses (which were more common than usual and probably occurred after the cows were banged up), I saw no unusual prevalence of infectious diseases in the herd. I cannot attribute any immunosuppression in their herd to "stray voltage" or any other electrical phenomena.

14. The Bellville herd did experience problems with bovine leucosis and lymph sarcoma. Those problems began after the Bellville's took in a large number of livestock from another dairy farmer.

A program was instituted to stop the spread of this disease in the herd, including measures such as stopping the use of common needles and dehorning equipment. I saw nothing which would lead me to believe that "stray voltage" caused or exacerbated any bovine leucosis or lymph sarcoma problems in the Bellville herd. Other stressors on the farm and nutritional difficulties could, however, have aggravated those problems.

15. Based on the level of management that I observed on the Bellville farm, I did not feel that the Bellville's dairy herd was producing less milk than it should have been producing.

16. I never saw any evidence that the Bellville's dairy livestock suffered from dehydration or starvation.

17. In summary, while the Bellville's did face certain challenges with their dairy herd, I have not seen or read anything

which leads me to believe that those challenges were caused or exacerbated by "stray voltage" or any other electrical phenomena.

18. I have nothing further to say in this Affidavit.

The affidavit from Dr. Risley was almost identically worded.

When I read this I felt so betrayed! Now I knew where Consumers was going to base their case. We were going to have to defend ourselves on all of the things that had been pinpointed in this affidavit. We had MSU do the rations (nutrition) for the feed on our cows and then we fed it. That did not stop the cows from dying or having displaced abomasums (twisted stomachs), lameness, milk fever, or ketosis. So if one of the best universities in the nation can't stop the health issues with our cows, how are we supposed to stop it? I was so hurt. Here was someone we considered a friend as well as our veterinarian, Tim had borrowed our camper one summer.

Dr. Risley had come to our daughter's wedding reception. To have them go over to the enemy and agree to this was an act of treason. I'm sure that it was written by Consumers and they just signed it, because the wording "other electrical phenomena" is one of Mr. Reynolds's favorite phrases. It points out the areas we keep going over in our depositions.

I could have handled them not wanted to support us, but to lend their hand to Consumers hurts beyond the capabilities of anyone understanding the depths of betrayal I feel. When we found out that we had Bovine Leucosis, I talked to the veterinarians who had the most experience with this disease and followed the practices, not using single needle for shots, disinfecting the tattoo equipment that our veterinarians used on each animal, and every cow had a new gloves used on her at examination time. We were the only farm that did this in our area. The West Branch veterinarians we used did not do this on any other farm. Now they want to take credit for it. They brought MSU up to our farm and sat in on the meetings we had at our farm. They very well knew we followed the recommendations that were given to us.

We not only have lost our way of life, we have lost good friends who are afraid that the stigma will rub off on them if they associate with us. Now we have to fight for our credibility and to deal with this tactic.

In the summer of 1999 Tim Eyth had written a letter that read:

To Whom It May Concern:

There has been a perceptible decline in health and production of the Bellville herd over the last several years.

There has been a dramatic increase in cow mortality to such a degree that Bellville's can no longer produce enough replacement heifers to maintain the size of their herd. We do know that the herd has an infection rate of approximately 50% with Bovine Leucosis. A large number of animal have died due to this disease in the last six months (approximately).

Bovine Leucosis is a common disease but accompanied by a low rate of transmission and a very low death rate. We feel that both the rate of transmission and death rates is due to presently unknown factors which have caused immunosuppression, decreased resistance to infection. So far infectious disease factors, such as BVD and Johnes, have all come back negative.

We are attempting to determine any factors which would add stress to this herd, but so far have been unable to identify any.

Historically, Bellville's have been good daily producers, exhibiting excellent management skills, with good cow health and accompanying production. Mortality figures were never high and health problems were similar to other well-managed herds.

Sincerely,

Timothy H. Eyth, D.V.M.

Until the affidavit showed up, we had no idea our veterinarians would turn against us. Our attorney, David Aldrich, said he looked forward to having them on the witness stand. At this point I was more hurt than angry.

Sheryl Krantz has decided to sell her cows. Her cancer is progressing. We have discussed where you move to get away from the influence of electricity. She is the one who had chopped straw on our field that has the pathways in it. About two weeks after she had been in that field her cancer came back and she hasn't been okay since.

The doctors had asked her if she lived by a large electrical line, and when she told them she lived one quarter mile from a transmission line, they told her to move. Hopefully, she will be okay. She doesn't know what to do with her life either, but she is trained as a massage therapist and she will try to do that and keep her farm land. I hope everything works out for her.

So many people whom I have talked to, have medical conditions along with sick cows. You just have to wonder if it is connected! If so, how do we get someone to take it seriously and make the utility companies change? Why do people have to get sick and die? I know we have to educate, but it takes so long!

CHAPTER 27

MAY–AUGUST 2002

O nce again, we are at the Consumers Energy annual meeting. As I do each time I come, I ask them when they are going to upgrade the utility lines that run in front of my house, that have been in place since the 1930's. As usual I get the standard run around. One lady says to me after the meeting, "Please don't stop coming. I come each year just to hear what you say to them." Sometimes I wonder if it is worth the hassle, but then I remember all the people who have been affected by this issue. If I stop, no one will remind Consumers that there is still a problem out there!

Things have a funny way of working, and as I have said before, God is leading in His own direction. Farm Credit is pushing us again. They will not restructure our loan so we can meet our payment and are back to insisting we sell our equipment. If we do that, we will not be able to farm at all. So we have agreed to put the land up for sale, pay down the debt and continue farming.

We have a friend who went to school with George Bush—not the President. He sells Real Estate, but you should have heard the operator when I called information to get his number. The ironic thing is that this George Bush's family was the one I have talked about before. They had problems with electricity on their farm and sued Consumers Energy. They were the ones that the Judge locked the court room and sent someone to Jackson for all the information on their farm. They were awarded $6 million dollars and his dad died at the age of fifty-two. The son came up to our farm. It was hard for him; it brought back too many memories as we each had the same experiences with Consumers Energy. But he would list our farm.

And he told us about his boss, Mr. Bolhon, who had worked with their farm dealing with Farm Credit and maybe he would help us.

We have made a new life for ourselves. We are busy with planting crops and harvesting hay. Kay, our youngest daughter, likes to show horses, so she has been going to horse shows with some friends. She must be pretty good; she brings home a lot of blue ribbons. She has earned them. She does it all by herself. We don't know much about horses.

Fall brings another farm sale. Wranglers at West Branch have decided to sell their cows. They sued Consumers Energy, received a settlement, but whatever Consumers was suppose to fix, they did not. Phil says that he can raise calves on the other side of the road, but the minute he brings them over by the cows, they die. They are tired of the struggle. When does it stop? Our Richland Township no longer has any milk cows in it. There are an awful lot of vacant farm buildings in our area. I don't know if any one will ever milk cows in our area again. With September here, we are going to have the long awaited and anticipated case before the Public Service Commission to testify for the Attorney General. Maybe we can get something accomplished now.

CHAPTER 28

SEPTEMBER–DECEMBER 2002

Our long awaited hearing in front of the Public Service Commission has arrived! Attorney General Frank Kelly brought the suit against Consumers Energy about five years ago, but it sat on a shelf until Attorney General Jennifer Granholm took it up. After a couple of years of investigating, we are ready to proceed. Last week Michael Moody, the attorney of record, called to ask me if I thought other farmers might want to talk at the hearing. I said yes, see what he could do. After discussions with the Judge and Consumers, Michael told me Consumers said "There was no way she (meaning me) was going to get her way!" Well, we'll see about that.

Monday, September 16, 2002, we started the hearings in front of Administrative law judge—Daniel Nickerson, Attorneys for Consumers Energy James Brunner and Robert Franzinger, Attorney Michael Moody worked on behalf of Attorney General Jennifer M. Granholm, and Michael A. Nickerson today for Steven D. Hughey, who represents the Public Service Commission.

Mr. Moody began "I know we talked off the record about Rule 207, and I know some of the farmers are here that wanted to make an oral request or motion for that type of statement. So I just want to pass it along, and I think there's a farmer that might want to make the request."

With no objections from Consumers Energy, (a little hard to do when there were a couple of TV cameras taping the procedure), I got my way, the first head to head Consumers and I would make during the fourteen days of testimony. The farmers were going to get to tell their stories for the record.

Because it is so important to get their stories out there, I'm going to write what was in each one's testimony.

The first farmer was my husband, Brian Bellville: "I am here today to tell you what is happening to our area of Ogemaw County. We are serviced by Consumers Energy from a two-circuit ungrounded substation. The delta lines that our circuit comes from also services our elementary and high schools.

"After a new 76,000-square-foot school and five hundred computers were added, it resulted in a large nonlinear load. A sewer system as well was added to the circuit coming to our farm.

"We experienced problems with equipment failure, motor shutdown or motor burned up. The sewer system has the same problems with the motors burnout, which continues today.

"The Public Service Commission ordered Consumers Energy to do testing on our farm. The week they were coning to test, the voltage changed in the primary neutral. It was being measured with a portalogger on the primary neutral. Consumers chose not to test after we asked for a copy of the test results. The voltage then changed back when they did not test.

"The voltage would change again two months later when Consumers was notified through the Attorney General's office that testing was being done on our farm. The testing started on Wednesday, but Consumers was not notified until the following Monday. Once again the voltage changed after Consumers knew they were being monitored but would not stay down. It would spike.

"The testing would show that we received voltage drops below the 114 legal limits to 106 volts. There would be a question of whether the meter was five volts low, but if you add five volts to 106, you still get 111, well below the 114 legal limits.

"As a result, Consumers brought their meter for a week, during which the voltage dropped below the legal limits 162 times. We were also keeping track of the times when our equipment would shut down. That happened so often that we ended up generating our own electricity. At this time, we called Consumers out. We had spent eighteen months asking testing to be done on current in the ground by an oscilloscope. That was never done.

"Consumers were told about the shocks my fifteen year old daughter and I were receiving from our equipment. They just ignored us. Our neighbor was getting shocks also, and Consumers moved her primary neutral to get the voltage out of her barn.

"During the last one and a half years Consumers Energy has replaced five transformers within a two-mile radius of our farm, one transformer having been replaced twice in the last year. As a result of the change in our operation, our electricity usage dropped off and the voltage on the primary neutral dropped almost in half. Our neighbor's electric bills, who are big electricity users, dropped $100 a month.

"When voltage goes down, current goes up, and electric meters measure current, Consumers does not have much incentive to fix low-voltage problems when they are making money off their consumers.

"The CYMDIST program run on our substation shows our circuit to have voltage drops on either side of our farm at 108 to 110 volts. By the time it completes the five-mile circuit, it has dropped to 104 volts. This is before we pull a load off the lines.

"In the fall of 2000 the portalogger picked up voltage of 25 volts after Consumers had worked on our substation on a Friday. It ran 25 volts until Monday.

"This summer on July 28th we were without electricity from 4:24 A.M. until 11:00 A.M. During that time the voltage on the logger registered twenty-five and a half volts until 2:30 P.M. Our side of the substation was not working. Where did the voltage come from? There was an ozone release, a terrible smell like burning oil at the substation. Consumers did not fix broken-down grounds or floaters on the lines near our house until two years after they were told about them, and there is still a tree on the lines that's been there for three summers.

"Consumers have put in an extra neutral line in parts of our area but only have two places on our substation, one coming from a school part way before they dump the voltage in the ground, the other from a residential area dropping that voltage in the ground as a neutral line goes back to the substation.

"Consumers have put in several miles of grounded delta line to a farm from a school so that the farm would not have stray voltage problems. They just hang you out to dry. Thank you."

The next farmer was Michael Vandenberg: "I take the position the same as what the Attorney General's office does.

"We had testified to the Stray Voltage Task Force meeting many years ago back in '93, and here we are coming up almost on ten years, and the Commission really hasn't got much done, and that's where a lot of us farmers are taking a position. Here it is—ten years and nothing's getting done.

"And one of my biggest concerns was the trees are still growing in the power lines and nobody's come out to trim them, and we've made several comments to Consumers Power Company to trim them on a regular basis and we're still getting nowhere.

"And one of our other problems was a farmer down the road from us just put an irrigation system in this last year, and I know one of the farmers on the other side of us. Consumers sent a letter that the irrigation system could possibly cause stray voltage on the system. We hadn't been notified from Consumers that this new system being put in that would cause us any problems.

"And so my concern is that we need more testing out there on our area to see if the trees are still causing problems, because we're experiencing problems on our farm health wise with us humans and our animals. We're still seeing problems with high CBKs, which is an indicator of electrical injury, and that was from the doctors out of Minnesota at the Mayo Clinic. Thanks."

Victor Mier: "I guess my experience with this, in '94 we burnt out and we built a complete new operation to milk cows, and lo and behold, I did not know it for four years, I bought cows and buried cows. When I finally realized what the problem was, I'd been ridiculed of everything there is by a lot of the people in this room, and when you find out what it is and you try to rectify it and you're willing to work with people—I've offered my farm to be a test farm because it was a complete new operation—nothing has happened.

"So consequently, I'm out of business and broke, but in the meantime I've done a lot of testing. We can turn the farm completely off, and there's electricity there. If my farm is completely off and there's electricity there, where's it coming from?

"We run for a year and a half on generator. While I run the generator I never had a computer shut down, and when we was on the utility company's, we constantly had computer problems. I mean it was a daily thing to be working on our computers.

"So I just feel that somehow things have got to take a different turn, and we've been working on this and I was told it was going to get fixed, it's going to get fixed, and I keep being told there's no problem. Well, somewhere along the line there's a problem because there's too many of us suffering, and that's all I have to say about it. It's a shame that we're suffering. Thank you."

John Roslund: "I have to agree with Mr. Vandenberg. We were here back in 1993, and I can't see where anything has changed, anything has gotten any better.

"We're out of business. I have no inclination of going back into business milking cows if I have to put up with what we've put up with. I feel like I have to be careful with what I say, and I guess that's part of our upbringing as being farmers because I think we were naïve and that this is boiling down. It's been a political problem. It's been a big money problem, big business, and I don't know. I guess the first time where we saw it was something on 60 Minutes and Mr. English was on it, and I guess that was in 1991.

"I have here the Judge's decision from our Circuit Court in Gratiot County, and it said that we should have known, we should have known, the farmers should have known from whenever we started to see problems with the cows. And I have to disagree with that. We pushed it, we pushed it all the way to the Michigan Supreme Court, but we couldn't get in because we didn't appeal soon enough, and we tried to do a leave to appeal, but it seems that our case lacked merit.

"And it really irritates me because I see people that are still facing the same problems that we had, and at that time I don't mean to attack you, Mr. Nickerson, but I remember seeing you on the news out of Saginaw—I believe it was Channel 5—and you said that 'We had a hearing tonight or today and it was about stray voltage, but no farmers showed up, so there must not be a problem with stray voltage.'

"But it was always a hard thing to get recognized that there could be a problem. If you talk to an electrician, they didn't understand it; they didn't know anything about it. If you called

Consumers at that point, they didn't seem to offer any explanation on why things could be happening.

"And then getting back to the Michigan Public Service Commission, I don't know how many phone calls I made, how many letters I wrote trying to get someone to investigate, and they said can't do it. And finally, when we did get somebody to investigate, they sent up someone that wasn't qualified, didn't know how to run the equipment, and yet we get a decision from a judge that says 'You should have known.'

"I guess that's what irritates me more than anything, and here it is ten years later and we're out of business, and like I said, I don't want to go back into it because I wouldn't want to go through this baloney anymore. Thank you."

Mr. Arlen Walt: "I could stand here and talk for days. The Attorney General's office has been working very closely with my farm. If you have any suspicions as to what has ever happened on my farm, just go through some of the documentation that they have.

"I built my new facility ten years ago. April of '92 I started milking in it, and yet to this day when I have to milk the cows myself—I have a lot of employees—but when I have to milk my own cows and see them cows come through that parlor one by one gimping and limping, hardly being able to move, and I've been dealing with this for ten years knowing what I'm dealing with. It's one thing when you have a problem, you address it, and you cure it. I have a problem; I know what the problem is. And there's nothing that is being done about it.

"Many things have changed over the past ten years, things that were suggested that I've changed. Just anything that people would surmise that could be a cure, I had implemented.

"Working with the Attorney General's office, if it hadn't been for them I wouldn't be where I am at today. It is a fraction of a bit better, but I'm saying a fraction.

"The best thing that has happened is for eight years I have struggled with low voltage along with stray voltage.

"Low voltage was a ten-horse motor would only last me nine months. Nine months I would replace a ten-horse motor on the farm. When they wee starting up and running, they would be so hot you could not put your hand on them without burning your hand instantly. They were running that hot because of the lower voltage.

"Like I said, the Attorney General's office has all of the documentation, everything, records that was taken, to prove how low it was.

"In the process, we were able to convince Consumers Energy to separate the line in front of my farm. Now I am fed from Coopersville which is just two miles straight east—the lines are a little newer, a little better—versus where I was being fed from the west which had to go all the way to Nunica, which went through the back roads, cross-country through lines which have not been changed since they were put up.

"There are so many splices and so forth from wind damage that had occurred in the past seventy years that it's amazing that they even stand up when you get back through there in the back roads.

"Anyhow, they changed me, split the line, so now I'm being fed from Coopersville. I have a better supply of power since that time, two and a half years ago, I believe. I have not replaced a single motor, not even a capacitor for a motor. That part has helped.

"My neighbor, neighboring dairy farmer, was over just ten minutes before I left to get cleaned up to come here today. He had just had a dealer come out and replace a big motor on his farm. He is only probably 1000 feet to the west of me, but he is still on the old line going back to Nunica substation, the substation I was on. He is still experiencing the same things I was as far as motors, motors burning out, running hot. He cannot touch them.

"Just a simple thing of upgrading the lines, getting these things—but nothing has been done—like the gentleman said, nothing has been done—ten years this has been going on knowingly, and nothing has been done.

"On the farm I am recording daily in the literature—you'll read there that anything over 10 millivolts affects dairy cows. On the best of days, I have 40 millivolts. That's on the best of days in a twenty-four hour period.

"Yesterday I wrote down, logged it into the computer. It was 475 millivolts. And you wonder why farmers are going out of business. I am one of the very few that are still struggling to keep going.

"Around my area, if you were to count up all of the dairy farmers that were there within a fifty year period, everybody is out, has gone out of business.

"And I'm just asking you, please, we here as dairy farmers are only representing a fraction of the people that the utility companies is affecting. This room would be packed full if it would be a rainy day. But as you can tell, it's a beautiful harvest time. It is optimum time to harvest crops. And I too should be home harvesting. But I would like, if there's any way possible, I would like to prevent the power companies from harvesting my cows. Thank you."

Leroy Roslund: "I didn't know that I would be able to say anything. I don't know how many meetings we have been to down here and we haven't been able to say what was on our minds. But I have one thing to say. That I just believe that Consumers Power Company is afraid to repair and fix what is wrong.

"When we first noticed that we had problems, they told us that we were our own problems. But then we spent $17,000 testing of our own money to find out where the problem was coming from.

"When we did find out where it was coming from, it took—after it was thrown out of Circuit Court in Gratiot County—it took Consumers Energy five and a half months to give us our own transformer so that we could be relieved of the problem.

"Now, I just believe that Consumers is afraid to upgrade and do anything because that's proof that they have done us real damage. Thank you."

Ms. Marilynn Momber (Michigan Farmers Union): "I have been around several of these farmers and I have witnessed the documents that were a part of this court, and I have reviewed them. I have talked to people in the area that have had the same problems and I have heard this all over the state.

"And I wish to read from the Michigan Farmers Union's stray voltage article: "We request that Michigan Farmers Union make it a top priority to urge enforcement of Sec. 21, General Requirement Rule 215-B of the National Electric Safety Code which prohibits the utilities from using the ground as the sole conductor for current. This affects the future of dairy and live-stock agriculture and health and people of rural America.

"All manufacturers of electronic or other equipment that produce nonlinear loads be required to install harmonic filters as a standard part of the equipment to eliminate harmonic currents from returning on neutral wires to the substations.

"Approximately sixty-five to seventy-five percent of the electric current in the electric distribution system returns to the substation through the earth, and only twenty-five to thirty-five percent return on neutral wire wherever the closed delta system is not used.

"Therefore, we request that anything that obligates the utility providers to improve the system and to return all electricity on the neutral return, and they should not use the earth as a return pathway to the substations. Thank you.'"

At least these farmers got to voice their opinion, whether it will do any good or not. I hope that these proceedings will be able to break the log jam, and we will be able to get some ruling so that Consumers and other utilities will have to upgrade their service in the rural areas of our state. I guess what really bugs me is that the farmers that were here today are just a few of the many who filled this room in April of 2000, when we had standing room only. The despair that you feel in their voices when you hear them talk is incredible! I guess I can't imagine being able to sit in a room and hear these stories and not be moved, but the Consumers people just doodle and patiently wait for them to complete their speeches so they can get started to rip the witnesses apart.

William English was the first witness for the Attorney General. He was a licensed professional engineer and stray voltage consultant. He had done a lot of work trying to help farmers. There are still a few people on both sides who go head to head on court cases and who testify against each other in Michigan and others states like Wisconsin or Iowa. I won't go into detail on each testimony because it was very technical, but each of the Attorney General's witnesses told how Consumers was hurting farms and farm animals. Of course, Consumers witnesses told how good the utility wires were and how the farmers just did not know what they were talking about.

CHAPTER 29

My testimony was next. When we got down to Lansing that morning, we walked in and met Mr. Reynolds, Consumers attorney who had done our depositions in Lansing. He greeted us with "Guess who wrote the questions for today?"

I said, "Who?"

He said "I did." He smiles like the Cheshire cat in Alice of Wonderland. Now that was supposed to make me nervous. They are pretty obvious! I guess I'm looking forward to this; it will be the first time I will go around with Consumers attorneys. Let the games begin. So we moved into questioning.

The first question asked: Ms. Bellville, according to the testimony which was just bound into record, you filed your direct testimony and exhibits on March 15, 2000; is that correct?

Answer: Whatever the date in there is.

Question: That date would reflect March 15, 2000. Several months after that you and your husband filed a lawsuit against Consumers Energy in the Ogemaw County Circuit of West Branch; is that correct?

Question: That lawsuit essentially was seeking monetary compensation for the loss of your herd and other compensation because of stray voltage, earth currents, transients, harmonics, and other electric phenomena; is that correct?

Answer: The lawsuit states what it was. I don't have the lawsuit papers in front of me.

Question: But the terms that I've just used, would those be fairly representative of the electrical problems that you're claiming in that lawsuit?

Mr. Moody: Well, I think, your Honor, I object. She stated that the complaint speaks for itself.

Judge Nickerson: Overruled. You may answer.

Answer: Without having the complaint in front of me, I'm not sure exactly all the things that are listed in it. Some of those certainly are.

Question by Mr. Dempsey: In general we could agree that your complaint talks about electrical phenomena that were causing harm to your dairy operation.

Answer: That word is used.

Question: As part of your civil lawsuit, did you recall a time when Consumers Energy asked the judge in West Branch to defer action on that case and refer that case to the Michigan Public Service Commission?

Mr. Moody: I object to the relevance and going into Nancy Bellville's separate lawsuit against Consumers Energy since it's not really part of this case.

Mr. Dempsey: Your Honor, the witness has filed a lawsuit against Consumers. She is a witness in this case covering the same types of issues, the same type of phenomena which you Honor is going to be asked to rule upon. And many of the experts in this case are also appearing in that case on behalf of the Bellville's and Consumers Energy. Indeed, some of the testimony which you'll be hearing later in this case from witnesses both for Consumers and the Attorney General reflect work done on the Bellville farm.

Mr. Moody: Your Honor, I don't object to him asking questions about things that are brought up in here, but general questions about her testimony and stuff, about what's taken place in the complaint, and would seem to be irrelevant as to what was filed in this case. I mean there are principles that apply for both. He's free to ask those. There's going to be a lot if overlap, obviously, but I think questions about the complaint itself and how it's working through the system and what it's doing and what they're arguing about, that would seem to be inappropriate and irrelevant anyway.

Mr. Dempsey: Your Honor, Ms. Bellville said, without me holding her to exact terminology in the complaint, that she doesn't have a copy of the complaint in front of her, that she would agree that electrical phenomena was discussed in that complaint. I think she's already moved beyond that in her testimony.

Judge Nickerson: All right. I agree with Mr. Moody. I don't see the relevance to the fact that this witness has a circuit court action either filed or pending. I fail to see the relevance at this point. Sustained.

I just sat there and watched the fur fly. The two attorneys got a little heated up. Consumer's Mr. Dempsey was a little hot under the collar. This should be interesting to say the least. Because this may be a little entertaining I'll go word for word from my testimony.

Question by Mr. Dempsey: In preparing your testimony for this case, did you read all of the documents that were produced by Consumers Energy in response to Attorney General questions?

Answer: No. I have not read the entire multitude of material that Consumers Energy has given the Attorney General's office.

Question: Do you remember what you have read?

Answer: Some of what I have read I might be able to remember.

Question: What have you read, by way of example?

Answer: I have read the file that Consumers has on our farm.

Question: Was that the file used by you to prepare the chronology which appears in your exhibit, Nancy Bellville 1?

Answer: No

Question: What was used to prepare Nancy Bellville?

Answer: My memory.

Question: Any written documents to back up your memory?

Answer: Yes.

Question: What kind of written documents?

Answer: There were calendars that we kept in the barn that different events were recorded on. There were feed charts that were kept. There were health records that were kept.

Question: How did you come to be involved as a witness in this case?

Answer: When we developed problems, another farmer in the area had been talking to the Attorney General's office and they brought—he brought Marty May over to our house, and we discussed some of the things that were happening at our house. And as the months went on, we became involved in this—my testimony became involved in their complaint.

Question: And it developed that you volunteered to offer testimony in this case? Or were you asked by the Attorney General's office?

Answer: I volunteered.

Question: Your Exhibit Nancy Bellville 1 indicates a chronology of different people and organizations visiting your farm beginning in 1998 with Consumers Energy continuing on page 2 with January 1999, Mr. Durst from Michigan State and other individuals, and followed by a number of events and visits by Michigan State Extension staff and various employees of Consumers Energy, finally culminating in a visit by staff engineer from the Commission in 2000. Is that a rough summary of the events?

Answer: That's a rough summary. There's some you've left out.

Question: What I left out is also contained in Nancy Bellville 1?

Answer: Yes.

Question: Without holding either one of us to a precise number, is it true that between 1998, in December of that year, and 2000, that Consumers made some eighteen visits to your farm, either by themselves or in conjunction with other individuals like Mr. Durst from Michigan Extension?

Answer: I don't remember them being there when Mr. Durst was there. They did make several trips out there. As to how many times, I would have to count them up. So I won't commit to a number of times. They did come, yes.

Question: And they came both to your farm for various inspecting purposes and testing purposes; is that correct?

Answer: Yes.

Question: And the Consumers employees also came to visit the Consumers poles and lines and inspect those facilities in the general area of your farm; is that also correct?

Answer: I know of one visit that I saw them drive by. Other than that, I don't know how many times they might have driven by to inspect lines.

Question: As part of your preparation for your testimony, did there come a time when a representative of the Attorney General's office came to your farm and set up a fluke event recorder to do some testing?

Answer: The Attorney General's office plugged in an event meter on our farm.

Question: And according to your chronology that apparently took place sometime in the fall of 1999; would that be approximately correct?

Answer: Either in the fall of 1999 or early 2000.

Question: Was the Attorney General the only agency that set up the event recorder at that time and did the monitoring?

Answer: For the event recorder?

Question: yes.

Answer: yes.

Question: I assume there came a time when that information was downloaded and taken by the Attorney General to the office, correct?

Answer: Yes.

Question: Do you know if information obtained from that event recorder was eventually turned over to Dr. Hillman for his analysis?

Answer: I have no idea. You'd have to ask the Attorney General's office.

Question: Was that event recorder supposedly set up to monitor electrical events that were allegedly causing harm to your dairy livestock?

Answer: My understanding of an event meter is it only monitors electricity on the line.

Question: Did the Attorney General do any monitoring of electrical events which might be affecting your herd?

Answer: No. Dave Stetzer did.

Question: As part of your testimony you have included as Nancy Bellville Exhibit Number. 2, copies of the staff report to you regarding their visit to your farm; is that correct?

Answer: yes.

Question: The letter from Mr. Whale, which appears as the first two pages of Nancy Bellville Exhibit 2, attempted to address three questions which gave you concern. Number 1, the grounding of the Consumers substation was improper and should be improved; Number 2, you believed that you needed a larger transformer to serve your farm; and Number 3, there was a missing ground wire from the farm transformer back to the substation. In the course of this report to you, Mr. Whale addressed those concerns. Do you have any criticisms of Mr. Whale's answers to your three concerns?

Answer: Yes.

Question: What criticisms do you have?

Answer: In Mr. Whale's report, one of the questions that I had was the fact that staff came up with Consumers and Consumers did all the measurements. Staff did not do any measurements themselves. In the business that I was in, if we had a tank of milk that was antibiotic suspected, the State of Michigan did not allow us to test our own tank of milk and state whether it was O.K. or not. My comment to them was, it's like asking the fox to guard the henhouse. There should be an independent agency who takes measurements to do that. At one point in time Consumers was told by the PSC we needed a bigger transformer, and they simply ignored it.

Question: On page four of Nancy Bellville Exhibit Number 2, there begins a memo from Mr. Paytash and Mr. Derkos to Mr. Whale detailing their visit to your farm; is that correct?

Answer: Yes.

Question: Is it your testimony that Mr. Paytash or Mr. Derkos, being trained engineers, were incapable of making observations and forming conclusions without the need to do their own independent testing?

Answer: When Mr. Paytash or Mr. Derkos, came to our farm, we requested of them to take some measurements at our farm, and they could not do so because they did not have equipment with them to do it. What I am simply saying is, the equipment and measurements were taken totally by Consumers Energy.

Question: Does not the memo from Mr. Paytash and Mr. Derkos to Mr. Whale reference the fact that they did no independent testing, Number 1? That's correct, we agree on that?

Answer: Yes, they did no testing of their own.

Question: And, Number 2, we also agree that the memo from Misters Derkos and Paytash to Mr. Whale say that they observed the Consumers measurements; is that correct?

Answer: That's what they say. I was not present, so I have no idea to know whether or not those are correct statements.

Question: And yet, based on their independent engineering judgment, which they detail in the memo to Mr. Whale, you are still of the opinion that they didn't do what you thought they were going to do. Would that be a fair criticism of—

Answer: My opinion is that we were not notified that they were even going to come up and do any measurements whatsoever. I would have hoped that there would have been an independent body doing it, outside of maybe either the PSC or Consumers doing testing, so that there would be an unbiased testing done.

Question: I understand that you and Consumers Energy have a disagreement as to what is happening on your farm. However, I am wondering about your apparent criticism about the bias or lack of bias of the staff. Apparently you don't feel that the MPSC engineering staff of the Electrical Division is capable of making an unbiased assessment of your farm and reporting back to their supervisors, who in turn reported back to you?

Answer: That's not what I'm saying. I'm saying that under the circumstances that I know of, when a request was made from PSC to Consumers to give us a larger transformer, that request was turned down. So what else am I supposed to believe?

Question: Apparently Mr. Derkos and Mr. Paytash addressed that very issue by finding, based on their observations and inspection of the data, that the transformer was adequate for the load on your farm.

Answer: I don't know that either of them ever was given an accurate load of exactly what was on our farm. The documents that were given to the PSC in the first place were about half as much as the actual load limits that were on our farm. When we contacted them and were told that, we sent down an additional document that listed the entire load that we were running on our farm. At that point in time was when PSC requested a larger transformer.

Question: Your earlier answers seem to suggest that the PSC staff could not do an unbiased investigation. And I say that because your earlier answer said that you would have wanted some independent agency besides the staff and Consumers to do an unbiased investigation. That leads me to conclude that you somehow believe the staff can't do an unbiased investigation.

Answer: I don't know staff well enough to come to that conclusion. I know what answers were given on our farm. I know that when we gave them the current information a different answer came to us than the one that's in the letter. And I know that that's what we were told. Other than that, I can't draw any conclusions. I'm not an electrical expert.

Mr. Dempsey: If I may have a moment, Your Honor.

Judge Nickerson: Yes, sir.

There was a discussion off the record. Mr. Dempsey and Mr. Reynolds held a conversation. I could hear Mr. Reynolds say ask her this, she doesn't know this. It was quite comical to watch them. I guess they just could not get the best of me and I wasn't giving them the answers they wanted to hear!

Question by Mr. Dempsey: Mrs. Bellville, did you keep any notes which let you identify which individual at the Commission said that you needed a larger transformer?

Answer: Yes.

Question: Who was that?

Answer: Lockie MacGregor.

Question: When did Mr. MacGregor tell you that?

Answer: In early spring of 2000. And he actually spoke with my husband.

Question: Let's go back to the chronology at Nancy Bellville Number 1. I believe there is a reference in March of 2002 from videotaping done on dancing heifers in January of 1999. Is that correct?

Answer: I don't see any reference to that in March.

Question: Is there a reference to that in January of 1999? Under January 1999, "Agra Volt tested. Brian took camera and taped cows moving in heifer barn." That would be a reference to Mr. Bellville videotaping in the barn: is that correct?

Answer: Correct.

Question: At the time your husband made that videotape, was there any simultaneous electrical testing being done at that time?

Answer: No. Shortly after he taped that, we took a meter down there and we measured two volts on a bolt on a wooden manger. When Consumers came back, we notified them. In Steve Wallenwine's deposition, he will state that he knew there was high voltage measured in that heifer barn.

Question: Were those heifers in that barn for some purpose?

Answer: That's where they were confined and being raised.

Question: Did you as part of your preparation for this case read Dr. Albright's report about that video in which he details several non-electrical reasons for the heifers moving around?

Answer: No.

Question: So you can not comment on the Albright report?

Answer: No.

Question: What testing on your farm did Mr. Perri and Mr. Wallman do?

Answer: They tested sag, swell, and harmonics. I'm not sure about transients.

Question: Who asked those gentlemen to come to your farm and do the testing?

Answer: We did.

Question: What was the reason for that?

Answer: Because by that point in time, that was the fall of 1999, we were searching for an independent electrical testing so we could see what was going on.

Question: Did you happen to review Mr. Wallman's test results which were included with his pre-filed testimony in this case?

Answer: I have reviewed the report that he gave us. I've not reviewed his testimony.

Question: What were your conclusions after reviewing Mr. Wallman's report?

Answer: Mr. Wallman's report picked up the fact that when we have sags and we have swells and we have harmonics present on our farm, that when the farm is turned off, the voltage does not drop to zero.

Question: Did you discuss this with Mr. Wallenwine?

Answer: Yes, I did.

Question: Did you discuss this report with any of your treating veterinarians such as Dr. Eyth or Dr. Risley?

Answer: Dr. Eyth is our primary veterinarian. Dr. Risley is a partner of his who only comes on an emergency basis when Dr. Eyth can't be there. We had some discussion about the fact that voltages were still there when the farm was turned off.

Question: When Agrivolt tested in January of 1999, did they provide you with a report of their measurements and their conclusions?

Answer: Yes.

Question: Didn't that report by Agrivolt conclude that they could find nothing wrong on your farm that could be attributed to the Consumers system?

Answer: No. That's not what the report says.

Question: Do you have any criticisms with the recommendations Michigan State made regarding your dairy farm and your dairy problems as detailed in your chronology?

Answer: You would have to point out which ones you're speaking of.

Question: Did Michigan State make recommendations about your feed?

Answer: Michigan State took responsibility for overseeing the feed that was being fed on our farm. Purina balanced the ration. It went down to Michigan State. Michigan State looked at it, said whether or not it could be fed. We fed it. It did not stop the health problems that we were experiencing.

Question: There is a reference on page three of your chronology, Nancy Bellville Number.1, July 30, 1999: It was determined that something had triggered the immune system to quit functioning. Dr. Eyth discussed this with Dr. Erskine, who is a Michigan State veterinarian, and apparently the two veterinarians concluded that BVD or bovine viral diarrhea might be a problem.

Answer: That was the discussion and at that time it was decided to test animals for BVD. All the adult animals were tested and none were found to be positive. So that was ruled out.

Question: Did Dr. Risley ever identify any non-electrical problems for the various herd concerns that you were experiencing?

Answer: As I've said before, Dr. Risley is not our primary veterinarian. He had some opinions that he stated along with various other people.

Question: Well didn't Dr. Eyth also advise you that in his opinion, based on his year of experience, that there wee a number of non-electrical concerns on the farm that he was concerned about that would account for the various problems your were experiencing?

Mr. Moody: Your Honor, I—

Answer: No.

Mr. Moody: Oh.

Answer: Dr. Eyth wrote us several letters stating that he was concerned with the immune system suppression on our farm but that we were good managers, we had had excellent production, and we had had problems with milk production but that it was not attributed to any of our management abilities.

Question: And it's your testimony that Agrivolt gave you their report. You evidently disagree with a comment in there that Agrivolt did not find any particular problem with the primary distribution neutral.

Mr. Moody, the attorney representing the Attorney General's office: I object, Your Honor. I think that the witness should have the document in front of her if they're going to—I think that she's allowed to have the document they're referring to. I think that's in the rules that the witness is allowed to review the document that he's questioning her on.

Mr. Dempsey: Well, let me rephrase it this way, your Honor:

Question: Did Agrivolt, to the best of your recollection, find any problems with the primary distribution neutral?

Answer: I would have to look at the document. My recollection of the document is that they said we had a problem with the utility company, which is exactly what they voiced when they were on our property. But without looking at the document itself, I'm not sure what you're referring to.

Mr. Moody: Your Honor, I'd like to also place an objection that Agrivolt is only mentioned once in Nancy Bellville-1, which is "Agrivolt tested." There's no testimony in any of direct or rebuttal about Agrivolt. I'm wondering—my objection would be relevancy. It seems like this might be something that they're trying to bring on with their complaint that they have—or that Ms. Bellville has with Consumers Energy. There's nothing really in her testimony about Agrivolt. Her testimony is more factual about situations, and is not anywhere except in Nancy Bellville-1 where she does a chronology of things that occurred, one of which "Agrivolt tested." That's all she ever talks about it. So I think we're going far afield with her testimony and I'd argue relevancy.

Judge Nickerson: I think the fact that Agrivolt tested is certainly relevant, based on her chronology. It's an event that happened and there is some data that presumably was collected from Agrivolt's testing. So overruled.

Question by Mr. Dempsey: Ms. Bellville, in response to your request—and if I may approach the witness, your Honor?

Judge Nickerson: Mr. Moody?

Mr. Moody: No objection.

Question: Here's a copy of the Agrivolt report dated January 20, 1999, addressed to Brian Bellville.

Answer: Yes.

Question: Now, before I ask you any more questions about this, let me show the same document to Mr. Moody.

Mr. Moody: Thank you.

Document shown to Mr. Moody by Mr. Dempsey.

Question: Mrs. Bellville, I'll direct you to the second page of
the report, which is Bates Number 002422. Do you see the
statement over here, "We have not found any particular
problem on the primary neutral utility"? Did I read that
correctly?

Answer: Yes, but they also did not do any testing on the
primary neutral. They only tested on the electrical service at the
barn. So I'm going to assume that that description is of the lines
and that weren't broken or corroded or whatever.

Mr. Dempsey: I have nothing else, your Honor.

Judge Nickerson: All right, thank you, Mr. Dempsey. Mr.
Moody, I have a few questions of this witness. I'd like to ask
them at this time so that you can cover it in redirect and Mr.
Dempsey can cover it in re-cross if need be.

Mr. Moody: All right, Your Honor.

Judge Nickerson: Ms. Bellville, on your proposed Exhibit C-
61, which is the chronology, on the third line there do you see
where it says "Sixty cows to as high as 136 cows and our herd
average too," and there's a number there, 21098. What does
that represent?

Answer: 21,098 pounds is what they call a herd average, and
that's—they take the monthly—we tested once a month, and
they take the amount of milk that you test once a month, and it's
a rolling herd average, and so it's done on a yearly basis that that
many pounds per day times that many number of days in a
month would equal out so much in a year.

Judge Nickerson: So that's pounds per day?

Answer: Its pounds per year per cow.

Judge Nickerson: All right. And further down under 1998, there's a statement "now have 450 computers instead of 50 we had in 1995." Is this a reference to PC computers, or what kind of computers are you talking about there?

Answer: This is a reference to PC computers. Two lines above that you'll see that in January of 1998 our elementary school— new elementary school, 76,000 square feet, opens.

Judge Nickerson: All right. I understand now. Thank you. What's your understanding of the use of the word "transients"?

Answer: My understandings of the use of the word "transients" are spikes that come through on the electrical utility side of the system which we have trapped in the monitoring devices that are on our farm.

Judge Nickerson: And you testified that when the MPSC staff came out, they did not conduct any electrical tests. Why would you have wanted them to conduct tests?

Answer: I guess I was disappointed because we were trying to find out what was going on and were not able to find independent, unbiased, not-paid-for-by-the-utility studies, not selling some kind of equipment to counteract whatever, and I was disappointed that the staff didn't have testing equipment because the hope was that they would be unbiased. But when all the numbers came from Consumers, that really concerns me greatly.

Judge Nickerson: O.K. And that leads to my next question. What did you find out in your attempts to locate someone you thought would be independent to conduct testing?

Answer: Well, I think it kind of tells a lot in the last exhibit where Dale Sheltrown says he will try and find us someone and he's our State Representative. At this point in time, he's never been able to find an independent that would want to step into the political controversial issue that we're all sitting here trying to address today. And I'm not sure, I know that's one of the things that's been considered, is to try and find someone independent. Nobody wants to answer the $64,000 question and put their reputation or whatever on the line to do so, and that's a terrible shame.

Judge Nickerson: So it's kind of a question of where do you go, who do you trust, who's good in the field, what the costs are, and those sorts of things?

Answer: And that's about the answer too, I guess: Who do you trust, where are they, if they sell something, how biased are they in their product that they're selling, who knows how to fix it. There are a multitude of Band-aid fixes. It's an extremely difficult, frustrating position to be in when you're a farmer who doesn't know anything about it and trying to find someone who does.

Judge Nickerson: Thank you very much.

Mr. Hughey Representing the Michigan Public Service Commission: Your Honor—

Judge Nickerson: Oh, I'm sorry, Mr. Hughey, yes sir. I knew you would speak up. Cross-examination, sir.

Mr. Hughey: I just have a couple of questions, Your Honor.

CROSS-EXAMINATION
Question by Mr. Hughey: Good afternoon, Mrs. Bellville.

Answer: Good afternoon.

Question: In response to counsel for Consumers' questioning, you indicated that Mr. MacGregor from the Commission staff had recommended a larger transformer for your farm; is that correct?

Answer: Yes.

Question: And I believe, if I understand the rest of your responses to questions, Mr. MacGregor didn't do any testing on which he based that recommendation did he?

Answer: Mr. MacGregor based his observations or his request on the load limits that we sent down to him and also requested that Consumers come up and do some testing on our farm. The day that he called me was a Friday, and when I downloaded the portaloggers that monitor the primary neutral, the voltage changed. And he informed me that Consumers would be there the following Friday to do testing. When they came, we had a disagreement because they wouldn't allow us to have the first downloaded disk so they did not set up their testing equipment. At that point in time, after they did not, the primary neutral voltage reverted back to what it was previously.

Question: But this was data—Mr. MacGregor's recommendation, if he recommended a larger transformer, was based on data that you supplied to him, not on—

Answer: it was data that—

Question:—not on data—excuse me. Just let me finish the question.

Answer: Okay.

Question: Not on testing that Mr. MacGregor had done; is that correct?

Answer: No. It was on load limits—the number of horsepower that we had running on our farm in regards to the size transformer that we had there.

Question: But I just want to make sure I've got the record clear here. It's data that you provided to him, not independent testing that Mr. MacGregor; did correct?

Answer: Correct.

Mr. Hughey: All right, thank you. I have no further questions, Your Honor.

JudgeNickerson: All right. Let's take a 15-minute recess and come back for redirect.

At this point I think I held my own, but they sure do try to get you to say something so that it makes them look good and you bad.

We will see what else they can come with to question me. The room is full with thirty people on Consumers side. There are four or five paralegals, and Mr. Dempsey, Mr. Reynolds, Mr. Wallenwine, Mr. Thompson, Mr. Schrandt, I guess I'm important or they want to intimidate me. You'd think by now they would learn that doesn't work with me! The wall next to Consumers is full of books, about hundred or more. It's pretty impressive. On our side there are about ten people and one paralegal and one attorney, Mr. Moody.

Judge Nickerson: All right, on the record. Redirect, Mr. Moody.

Mr. Moody: Thank you, Your Honor.

REDIRECT EXAMINATION
By Mr. Moody:

Question: Mrs. Bellville, during cross-examination by Consumers' counsel, there were several questions relating to testing that was done or a visit by MSU regarding feed and about what they had done on your farm.
    I think it's referenced in your Nancy Bellville-1, and it was discussed briefly about what MSU had done on your farm. Can you tell me what type of test MSU did on your farm or what they concluded?

Answer: MSU did medical testing. They could not find that we had any diseases present except for bovine leukemia, and the bovine leukemia that was found on our farm directly dated back to when a communication tower that is Consumers Energy's was put into operation.

Question: O.K. Also during cross-examination, I believe the staff or counsel for the MPSC staff asked a question about the data that you supplied to Mr. MacGregor at the PSC. The data that you provided to Mr. MacGregor, is that from a portalogger?

Answer: We have portaloggers on the farm, and when Mr. MacGregor told me that Consumers was going to come out and do testing, I downloaded the portalogger and the portalogger showed that the voltage had dropped significantly during the time that they were going to come out and test. I did fax that to him because he couldn't believe that the voltage would drop. It went up when they did not test. It was the second time in which the voltage dropped during use of the portaloggers that had been on the primary neutral for better than two years. They monitor the primary neutral which is Consumers' site, monitoring the voltage that goes into the ground. When we arranged to have testing done in June of 2000, the testing equipment, the Rustrack, was placed on our farm on a Wednesday, and through the Attorney General's office, Consumers was not notified until Monday that the testing was being done, and the voltage didn't change until after Consumers was notified that testing was being done on our farm.

So during that period of testing the voltage stayed down.

When the downloaded disk was given to Consumers, that's when the question whether—because the voltage showed that it sagged to 106 volts, at that point in time there was a question of whether the meters were five volts too low, and if you add the five volts to 106, it equals 111, which is well below the 114 legal limit volts.

So at that point in time Consumers decided to bring their own equipment and come out to test. The week that their equipment came out to test, there were 162 times during that week the voltage dropped below the 114 limit.

Question: And was that information that they provided to you?

Answer: That was information that came off the downloaded disk that they left at our farm.

Question: And you continued to use these portaloggers on your farm?

Answer: We continued to use the portaloggers on our farm, and we picked up a significant problem on the 28th of July of this year in which we had a thunderstorm that put the electricity out—

Mr. Dempsey: Your Honor, if I may object. If I understand Mr. Moody's questions–and I apologize for interrupting you in the course of a dialogue–but if we're into June of 2000, I think we're beyond the period covered by the scope of this hearing in terms of the prefiled and the rebuttal testimony. We're getting into testing which is beyond the scope of what time parameters we're dealing with, and I apologize, but I think the Court should be aware of that.

Mr. Moody: I don't know if my—it seems like most of the questions were regarding the portaloggers and I thought that asking her about what they're continuing to do on her farm would be within this case because Consumers kept talking about the current situation, what's happening now, and that was with other witnesses, but it seems to be the claim or the argument from Consumers' counsel is that we're talking about what's happening to Consumers' system now, and this is just her testimony about continuing portalogger data that she is retrieving. I think it's a natural addition to what she had said here. I know she's testifying from her personal knowledge on these portaloggers. I guess that would be my argument.

Judge Nickerson: Sustained. It's not relevant and it's beyond the scope of the question.

Mr. Moody: Ok.

Question: And, Mrs. Bellville, during the cross-examination that Consumers' counsel conducted there was some discussion about how many times Consumers Energy had come out to your farm. I know in Nancy Bellville-1 you list numerous times that they had come out to test for low voltage on your farm.

Answer: Yes. In June of 2000, that was when they tested, and the sags were 162 times during the week that they were there that the voltage went below the 114 limit.

Mr. Dempsey: Same objection, your Honor. It's beyond the scope of the hearing.

Mr. Moody: Well, they already asked how many times they'd come out, and I'm just asking what they did, what did they test for. That's within her testimony. I think it's Nancy Bellville-1.

Mr. Dempsey: But Nancy Bellville-1 begins on page 1 with a recitation prior to 1995, and it ends on page 8, with March of

2000, and the questions are now into June and the summer of 2000.

Mr. Moody: Well, the rebuttal was filed in—well, actually this year, January 2002.

Mr. Dempsey: But the rebuttal doesn't deal with the same issues that the direct deals with.

Judge Nickerson: I think June of 2000 is not encompassed by the direct and is not encompassed by the chronology. Sustained.

Question by Mr. Moody: Did Consumers ever test for low voltage during the time frame that you have in Nancy Bellville-1, Mrs. Bellville?

Answer: Yes, they did. The first time they came out in February of 1999, I believe it is.

Question: And do you know what the results of those low testing measurements were?

Answer: No, because the information that they left us with, although the graphs showed that there were high spikes and low spikes. But at that point in time we didn't understand what that was—they were able to give us a printout that would give us how many times the sags were and how many times the swells were. That didn't come until 2000, when we realized that we got another report that said that that information was in there. So the information was available in February of 1999. They chose not to give it to us on their report.

Question: And that information that was available is the low voltages that you're talking about?

Answer: Correct.

Question: How many? What were the numbers of low voltages? What were the results of those low voltages testing.

Answer: Well, the results of the low voltage testing done in

February, we don't have any idea because they did not give us that information. The only information I have from them on low voltage comes at a later date.

Question: There was discussion about, during the cross-examination by Consumers about the event meters that were downloaded?

Answer: I was there a couple of times when the event meters were downloaded.

Question: And who downloaded the event meters?

Answer: Marty May from the Attorney General's office.

Question: O.K. And did you learn anything from the event meters in the measurements that you saw?

Answer: Well, the event meters show the transients that were present. And there were a large number of high transients that showed up on the down loads that I saw.

Question: And again during the cross-examination by Consumers' counsel, there was discussion about the amount of times that Consumers Energy had to come out to your farm, which again is detailed in Nancy Bellville-1. Are there still issues that need to be addressed by Consumers Energy that need to be fixed?

Answer: Yes. All the times that Consumers came out to our farm they brought hand-held equipment. They never brought an oscilloscope to measure the ground current that was present on our farm. The Rustrack that was there was not an oscilloscope that measures ground current, even though we requested that they bring one.

At the present time there are still issues in our area. After they made an official visit last December for our lawsuit, within about four or five days, maybe a little bit longer, they were out and fixed a broken down ground, and they fixed floaters. One was on a hot line; one was on a neutral line. They still have not fixed a tree that's on our lines that they have known about for three years. They still have not fixed two broken down grounds that are within a mile and a half of us.

So there are—there's right now presently a broken insulator that's across from the substation. So there are still maintenance problems on our system that they have not addressed.

Question: O.K. And I know during cross-examinations counsel for Consumers Energy suggested that the PSC staff who had come out to measure at your farm had electrical background. Do you know whether the staff that came out, the two individuals that came out to your farm, do you know whether they have a degree in electrical engineering?

Answer: My understanding is neither of them holds a degree in electrical engineering, which is also not uncommon with the people that come on our farm from Consumers. You have to go a long ways up in Consumers to find someone who holds an electrical engineering degree. The ones that come out to our farm do not.

Question: And again talking about the portaloggers that were discussed earlier, you do have them monitoring, obviously, the primary neutrals as you stated, and the voltage from that primary neutral as entering the earth. What is the highest level of voltage that you've recorded?

Answer: The portaloggers max out at twenty-five and one half volts. We have maxed out the portaloggers twice. Once was in the fall of 2001, and once was this summer on the 28th of July when we had a thunderstorm that put the electricity out at the substation. And the substation, they tell me, had an ozone release because you could smell the burnt oil.

At that point in time the electricity was off on our side of the substation in our farm from 4:24 A.M. until 11:00 A.M., and we solidly monitored twenty-five and one half volts until 2:30 in the afternoon, when it dropped.

During the next week it spiked up and down and had twenty-five and one half volts several times until they did general maintenance the following week at the substation, and since then it's stayed down.

Mr. Moody: All right. No further questions.

Judge Nickerson: All right. Thank you. Recross, Mr. Dempsey?

Question by Mr. Dempsey: Mrs. Bellville, let me take you back to your answers which you gave in response to Judge Nickerson's questions. You mention that you were looking for somebody competent to do testing on your farm; is that correct?

Answer: I'm not sure how you define "competent."

Question: For example, did you have any problems with the testing done by Mr. McVeigh from the Michigan Milk Producers Association on your farm in '98 and '99?

Answer: Mr. McVeigh is not—has not been trained, that I'm aware of to do electrical testing, except showing a meter. He might have had a couple days of training. He's not an electrical engineer. He does not do anything except he's a milk inspector for the State of Michigan, so his qualifications are: What should be done to follow the regulations for the production of milk?

Question: Are you saying that you need to be an electrical engineer to be competent to do testing on your farm?

Answer: What I'm saying is that Mr. McVeigh used a fluke meter that's fifty percent accurate at the best, and has not been trained any more than me. You don't want to accept my testing or what I look at to test. I'm not different than Mr. McVeigh.

Question: So you would disagree with his testing in 1998 and 1999 as reflected in the MMPA report that he gave you for those months?

Answer: I wouldn't disagree that the voltage levels he saw there at that point in time were what he wrote down.
I also know that we took a fluke meter similar to his, took it down to our heifer barn and measured 2.5 volts on a bolt in a wooden manager.

Question: Do you have any disagreement with the testing done by Mr. Wallman and Mr. Perri in the fall of 1999 on your farm?

Answer: Mr. Wallman and Mr. Perri use a Rustrack. I guess I'm questioning what you're getting at. They did a report and the report showed that there were problems there.

Question: Well, the question was: Do you have any problems with their competency since you testified that you hired them to do the testing? Now, presumably you hired them because you thought they were independent and could do a good job for you. Or am I misunderstanding your testimony?

Answer: No. We hired them to do electrical testing on our farm and we received a report from them. They set up, according to MSU recommendations, just exactly the same as when Consumers came. I didn't disagree with what they showed either. It showed we had a problem on both of them.

Question: Did the report from Mr. Perri and Mr. Wallman indicate that some of their measurements indicated voltages that would have been at levels where a person or animal could be electrocuted?

Answer: I don't think I'm able to make an interpretation. I know what the graph showed, and the graph showed levels still present when the farm was turned off. But there also was an extremely high spike which came through at further testing on our farm that was also brought down to this courtroom and discussed between the AG's office and Consumers on testing that was done June 1st of 2000 also. And no explanation was given at that point in time where it came from, except it comes through on Consumers system.

Question: You mentioned the event recorder. When that was downloaded, the data from that recorder was downloaded, did there come a time when any of that data was lost and not downloaded?

Answer: You would have to ask the Attorney General's office because they downloaded that information and I wasn't always present when it was downloaded.

Question: Did you ever get anything from Mr. MacGregor stating that you should have a larger transformer?

Answer: No.

Question: In response to the Judge's questions, you still seemed to suggest, if I'm hearing you correctly, that the Commission staff somehow is not up to the job of doing the kind of independent testing you think ought to be done on your farm.

Answer: What I'm—

Question: Or am I misunderstanding what you're saying about the staff?

Answer: I think you're misunderstanding because when staff was at our farm, their comments to us were that they did not have equipment to test with, that we needed to contact our congressman in order to get enough money to buy testing equipment so that they could test on their own.

Mr. Dempsey: I have nothing else.

Judge Nickerson: All right. Thank you, Mr. Dempsey. Recross, Mr. Hughey?

Mr. Hughey: Maybe just one question.

RECROSS-EXAMINATION
By Mr. Hughey:

Question: I believe in response to Mr. Moody's question about the educational background of Mr. Paytash and Mr. Derkos, who visited the farm; you indicated that you didn't believe they were electrical engineers.

Answer: My understanding–what I have been told–is that one of them holds a mechanical engineering degree and not an electrical engineering degree. Other than that, I have not seen any background on either of the two people.

Question: O.K. So it's fair to say you're not familiar with what their educational—

Answer: No.

Question:—or training background is; is that correct?

Answer: No. That's correct.

Mr. Hughey: Thank you. I have no further questions, Your Honor.

Judge Nickerson: All right. Are there any objections to the admission of proposed Exhibits C-61 through C-63?

Mr. Dempsey: None from Consumers, your Honor.

Mr. Hughey: No objection, your Honor.

Judge Nickerson: All right. They are admitted. Thank you, Ms. Bellville. You may step down.

Mr. Moody: I think that's the only witness we have for today, ending with Ms. Bellville. Dr. Hillman is tomorrow morning.

Judge Nickerson: We have Hillman and Wallman scheduled for tomorrow morning, and then the afternoon is Mr. Wallman. All right. We're adjourned.

At 3:55 P.M., the hearing was adjourned until 9:00 A.M. on Wednesday, September 18, 2002.

As we were signing out of the Commission Building, Judge Nickerson was ahead of us. He turned around and said, "Mrs. Bellville, are you coming again tomorrow?" I told him we had a three hour drive one way, but I would return. He said, "I kind of thought you'd be back", and he laughed going out the door.

It had been quite a day. At first I thought we really were going to get into it with Consumers bringing up our lawsuit. I thought we might be on trial here. I figured out that Consumers was trying to get me to say I didn't think that the Public Service Commission was incompetent. When they could not get me to say that, they would move on to another subject. I don't think they accomplished anything today. Consumers' attorneys certainly are bulldogs!

It sure looks one sided with all of the lawyers on Consumers side and only one attorney on our side. Michael Moody has his work cut out for him. He has to cross-examine all of the Consumers witnesses himself, but Consumers is splitting up the AG's witnesses among about four to five attorneys.

CHAPTER 30

Victor and Rose Mier are staying in a campground in Lansing, so they can be at each day's hearings. But we have to make the trip back down to Lansing for the testimony of Dr. Donald Hilllman. Dr. Hillman is retired from MSU; he has worked on the economic losses on our case. He and Charles Goeke, a statistician, had received a lot of material from dairy farms in Michigan and Wisconsin. They had to write a program to correlate the incidences of electric events on milk production. We had an event meter, as did the others and the days that there were a lot of events, milk production went down. We kept records on how much milk went into the milk cooler for sale, how much we fed to calves, how much we dumped out because it was treated milk, how many cows we dried up because they were waiting to have their calves, how many cows had calves, when their milk was good to go into the milk cooler, how many cows died or were sold. A lot of information to correlate. All the farms pretty much showed the same thing. Having to write a program for this information and correcting it so as to only have the electricity affecting the amounts took about thirteen or fourteen tries. When the testimony was filed, they were on program two or three. As Dr. Hillman testified, it got very complicated with all the graphs, and Consumers wanted to use only the old programs instead of the new programs. They bulldogged him just like they did me. They made a big deal out of his work not being peer reviewed. He had sent it out to be reviewed but had not gotten anything back on it. Consumers just would not believe that farmers could know what is going on with their cows.

Frank Perri testified that Consumers expressed disinterest in purchasing a recently updated version of instrumentation it had been using to monitor stray voltage, even though the new model produced more accurate readings.

Larry Wallman testified about certain Consumers facilities that, in his view, exhibited inadequate workmanship or code violations and were contributing to stray voltage.

We missed these two testimonies, but these gentlemen were the ones that had done the electrical testing on our farm. I know that they had been working trying to get Consumers to change their system for a long time.

Dr. Andrew Johnson, a veterinarian from Wisconsin testified to the adverse health effects of stray voltage on dairy cows. I had talked to Dr. Johnson in the summer of 1999 and told him what we had tested for and what we were doing. He said we had done everything he would have had us do and did not have any more suggestions.

Dr. Martin Grahman, an electrical engineer from Berkeley California, discussed and critiqued some of the scientific literature related to stray voltage research and measurement techniques.

Alex Furo from Canada, a forensic and electrical engineer, testified regarding a theoretical basis for understanding stray voltage, which encompasses electrostatic and magnetic forces based on the field theory of electricity. Mr. Furo stated that field explains why animal experience electrical sensations in the absence of readily measurable voltage differences between two points of contact. Mr. Furo had been in our area and at our farm when he was visiting his cabin at Sage Lake about ten miles North of us and on our substation.

Dr. Kenneth Main, a veterinarian, testified regarding physical signs that livestock are being harmed by stray voltage. I had talked to Dr. Main the summer of 1999 when I was looking for anyone who could tell me something. All of the symptoms he described we had seen. I talked to him after his testimony was completed.

He had gone to school with Dr. Tim Eyth, our veterinarian. I asked him if Dr. Eyth had ever called and talked to him. His answer was no. I was disappointed; we had tried so hard to know what to do. I asked him how he had decided electricity caused problems. He told me you ruled out everything else and that left

electricity. I asked him why he believed electricity caused problems and he said you either believed or not. If you did not believe,
no one could change your mind. He had wished Dr. Eyth had
called him.

Next came Consumers witnesses Jack Albright-Purdue
University who had been to our farm, John Kaneene
Epidemiology at MSU, and Charles Foster from Wisconsin who
also had been to our farm and reviewed videotapes of livestock
movements filmed by Stetzer and testified that there was no
correlation between the animal movements shown on the tapes
and recorded electrical activity. Just like the video that my
husband had taken of our heifers stepping that Consumers said
was flies bothering them in January. They all had excuses as to
why the cows stepped. Michael Stringfellow from Arizona and
had been to our farm criticized the Attorney General's testing
methodologies.

Dr. Michael Lane had been to our farm and Wayne Leja, financial analyst employed by Consumers, and Edward Rothman,
Professor of Statistics at University of Michigan, testified that there
were mistakes and errors in the statistical analysis used by Dr.
Hillman to draw a correlation between electrical readings and milk
production records. As I had said before, Consumers would not use
the last reports of Dr. Hillman's. The earlier ones he had admitted
were not as accurate as Number 13 report. The witnesses concluded
that Dr. Hillman's conclusions were not reliable and that the data
did not demonstrate a statistically significant correlation.

Daniel Aneshansley had been to our farm and surveyed the
research that he and others had done to test the effects of stray
voltage and ground current on dairy cows. He concluded that
currents of less than six millamperes (mA) at a frequency of sixty
hertz (Hz) have no direct effect on dairy production, reproduction,
or health. The AG's attorney managed to trip him up on several
points.

Douglas Reinemann from Wisconsin described his stray
voltage research on dairy cattle and explained how electrical
shock can affect an animal's biological functioning. He summa-
rized the existing scientific research by observing that only a few
cows exhibit a behavioral response to electrical current.

Consumers attorneys tore Dr. Hillman apart for not having his research peer reviewed and not wanting to believe the farmers observations. Yet one of their witnesses quoted a study done where his student assistant reported that cows milked better if country music was played instead of rock music. When asked how they had determined that fact, he said that the farmers who milked these cows told him they stood better with country vs. rock music. That was pretty funny; it was okay to accept the farmers' word on cows' behavior, but when we told them our animals were stepping around, Consumers claims that flies were bothering them in January. Every time we as farmers tried to use an observation Consumers say it is not scientific. There certainly is something wrong with this picture.

Testifying for Consumers, Charles DeNardo and LaVerne Stetson who both had been to our farm described the regulatory proceedings and developments relating to stray voltage in Wisconsin and Minnesota, respectively.

Wayne Knoblauch, Cornell University, testified that average milk production in Michigan and Consumers' service territory was outpacing production in other states. Linda Erdreich, an epidemiologist, testified that stray voltage does not present a potential risk to human health.

Frank Denbrock, a consulting engineer, inspected the Consumers facilities identified in Mr. Wallman's testimony and determined that they complied with Code requirements. He had inspected our substation and said it needed to be grounded on the corners, which was not done.

John Dagenhart, another person at our farm, described the historical evolution of grounded systems with the electric utility industry and the changes in the Code that have facilitated their use. He further explained that the ground connections in a utility's multi-grounded distribution system regulate voltage surges by facilitating the clearing of ground faults (for example, when a phase wire breaks and fall to the ground) and providing protection against lightning strikes.

Richard Thompson, one of the people who came to our farm and was present when our daughter told them she was getting shocks off our equipment and he just ignored her and left as soon as they were done downloading their equipment that showed the voltage had dropped to a lower level of 107, well below the allowable limit, is a Senior Technical Analyst in Consumers' Agricultural Service unit. He explained the methodologies that Consumers uses when called upon to investigate a stray voltage complaint. Mr. Thompson had been a car salesman before he started with Consumers. As I said, no electrical engineers came to our farm. My husband went to MSU's school on Stray Voltage after we had problems and is certified to test for Stray Voltage. He is as knowledgeable as Consumers. More so, he has lived with the results and has no one to protect.

As I have noted, many of these people who had testified had been to our farm and as they testified our farm came up or our substation came up. Time and time again, the substation came up, they kept saying as that the substation report was absolutely accurate. That was beginning to really bug me. Before the last witness on Friday afternoon, I said to Michael Moody, the AG attorney that the substation report was not 100% accurate. It had a substation map in the report that was not our substation. As Mr. Whales who had written this report was the next witness I suggested he ask about the map. It really did not mean anything, but why not? When Mr. Whale took the witness stand, he stated that it would be impractical to eliminate all earth currents, which are an inevitable outcome of grounding electrical systems. He recommended that the Commission promulgate minimum standards for acceptable levels of stray voltage. Then he testified he had written our substation report and it was absolutely accurate.

Mr. Moody, the attorney for the AG, took over. He laid the report in front of Mr. Whales and opened to the page of the substation map which was not our substation. It said Oliver substation instead of Prescott. Mr. Moody asked for the name of the substation on the map. Mr. Whales looked at it and looked at it—He didn't say anything, just sat there looking at the page. Consumers started to look around. They did not have the report in front of them, and so Mr. Brenner, the Consumers attorney, turned to a paralegal to get the information. The only place it was available was as part of my testimony. It was in one of the 100 books on the wall.

By this time, a couple of minutes had elapsed. I had been helping the Attorney General's counsel retrieve papers, so I was sitting next to the Public Service Commission's counsel where I could see all the players. This was getting pretty hilarious. Consumers now has the book holding my testimony but cannot find the right page, so the AG counsel has to go over and turn to the right page. Consumers counsel looks at it and turns around to have Mr. Thompson come up and look at it. They flip through the pages of the report, about eight or ten and keep doing that a couple of times, looking at each other as though to say " Where did that come from?!" Mr. Whales still has not said a word and we're going on about five minutes by this time. I'm sitting there trying not to laugh aloud; the looks on their faces is incredible. This thing has all of a sudden taken on a life all its own! Finally, Mr. Moody says to Mr. Whales, "Does it say Prescott anywhere on that substation map?"

Mr. Whales hesitates, and then he answers "No". We could barely hear him.

Mr. Moody asks "Did your people tell you this was the wrong substation map?"

Mr. Whales, "No".

That ended the questions from the AG's counsel. Next came Consumers back again, "Mr. Whales, even if the report is not 100% accurate, you'd accept the report wouldn't you?"

Mr. Whales responded with "Yes."

Then Judge Nickerson asks Mr. Hughey representing the Public Service Commission if he had any questions. Mr. Hughey, who was beet red, asks Mr. Whale "Even if the report on the substation was not 100 % correct you'd still accept it wouldn't you?"

Mr. Whales reply was "Yes." That ended the day's testimony with no further questions. We would have one more day of testimony the following Thursday.

Mr. Moody, AG's counsel, came over to me and said, "I think you proved your point. It was a shoddy report."

As I said, this thing took on a life of its own. I knew I had Consumers between a rock and a hard place. I would not have touched that with a ten foot pole, but knowing the EGO that

Consumers has, they will have to come up with an explanation somehow. The lady who had been doing the recording the last two weeks was going on vacation and we would not see her again. I asked her what she thought and how we were doing. She said she thought that Consumers had found their match in me! My ego does not need to be stroked, but it made my day; it was nice to best them for a while.

CHAPTER 31

The next Thursday, we all came back for the last day of testimony. James Schrandt, who had sat at our kitchen table, had just retired from Consumers. He described Consumers' program for addressing the stray voltage concerns of its agriculture customers. Then Consumers started back in on the substation report. I knew they would not be able to leave it alone. The explanation was that within this report there were four or five pages that talked about ground resistance and this map of the Oliver substation was supposed to be part of that report. It sounded good whether or not it was true. Nowhere in those four to five pages was there any reference to Oliver substation.

The Attorney General presented written testimony from Duane Dahlberg a retired physics professor from Minnesota. I had met him at the Arlyn Walt farm several years before and had read about a lot of work done in Minnesota, another state that has a lot of problems. He addressed a wide range of scientific, technical and theoretical issues relating to electrical distribution systems that serve dairy farms.

Michael Behr, a forensic economist from Wisconsin, testified identifying misapplications of scientific methodology and flaws in research protocols exhibited by various Consumers witnesses. And William Peloquin, an employee of the Attorney General, discussed the rate making implications of stray voltage. The record was closed on October 10, 2002.

After hearing some but not all of the testimony on both sides, I would hope that a ruling would come in our favor, but if this goes like the rest it will go in Consumers favor. The Attorney General ran into a problem with one of the major witnesses.

Dave Stetzer from Wisconsin, who had done a lot of the electrical testing in Michigan and Wisconsin, decided at the last moment not to testify and so none of his work could be put into place and a great deal of the proof on what was happening on the farms could not be used. The Attorney General says that there was no prior notice that Mr. Stetzer might refuse to participate and when the Attorney General found this out and wanted to substitute testimony from Donald Zipse, it was not allowed. The Attorney General claimed that the testimony in question was crucial to establish Code violations and explain the significance of transients and harmonics, so that the Administrative Law Judge's refusal to permit a substitution of witnesses was prejudicial. Because Mr. Zipse's testimony was similar to Mr. Stetzer's, the Attorney General claims, Consumers would have incurred no more prejudice from the substitution than the Attorney General incurred when Consumers substituted Dr. Rothman as a witness for Richard Andrews. As with our case, it seems that each individual case has to start from scratch and learn as you go. On the other hand, Consumers just uses the same information on each case. As I sat there and listened to their witnesses, I heard the same statements that they had used on our farm. I have discovered that politics plays a part in everything and right is not always right when politics get involved. The Attorney General did a good job of presenting their case in spite of all the road blocks that were placed in their path. The Attorney who had started the case for the first two years had been moved to another department, and Michael Moody had received the material in April of 2002 to go to trial in September of 2002. That was a very short time to learn a very complicated case. He did a great job against the opposition, who had a great deal more experience with the material.

So another year closes with no more progress than before except that the general public and the legislators are more aware that there is a problem. We will see what next year brings.

Chapter 32

A nother year dawns to us. We are getting our routine down now, but we certainly have changed. Kay, our youngest daughter, will be graduating this year. For the first time in many years, we will have an empty house. I will miss having her around to help fill the endless hours that we now have without dairy cows. How life changes when you least expect it to.

We just have been informed by Farm Credit that they are going to call our loan. After three years, they still have not gotten our loan switched so we can meet the payments and now we're beginning to get the barns up on numbers of animals. When they reach 1400–1500 pounds in weight, we will be able to sell them). They just won't work with us and for some reason they have decided to pull the plug. We have been with Farm Credit for more than forty years and have always paid our way. We cannot get any more calves; what is in the barn will be all that we will be able to raise. They are successfully limiting our ability to continue to farm, but that seems to have been the cause of the "credit risk manager" ever since we sold the cows. When Farm Credit has a loan that they feel is at risk of not meeting payments, Farm Credit turns it over to their "credit risk manager". We could have made our payments if they would have redone our loan payments to meet our present income. The "credit risk manager" decided that Brian needed to retire. It didn't matter that we wanted to continue farming. Farm Credit is determined we are all done farming!

We have had the farm listed with the realty company for six months, but not had any hits on it.

We are going down to talk with Mr. Bohlen who owns the realty company we are using. He has gone to bat with Farm Credit before and we can't do it alone anymore. We need to see if he can negotiate something so we don't lose the whole farm. This is the same place most farms with electricity problems end up at; trying to salvage something. Most of the time, they lose.

After several months of negotiations we think we have an agreement, but we need to go to an attorney to make sure we have protected ourselves. I call an attorney in Bay City, Henry Knier. He is a bankruptcy attorney, which is not what we want to do. He was the attorney Diane Taliska had used when she tried to remove her cows. We had never met him, but we'll see what happens. He says that there are some changes that need to be made on the papers that Bohlen and Farm Credit have come up with, so we send them back to Bohlen, he sends the correction back to Farm Credit and all hell breaks loose.

We received a fax from the "the credit risk manager" at Farm Credit giving us by the end of the day to sign the paper as is or they would seize all of our assets within twenty-four hours.

That meant that they would come in and load up all the cattle on the farm and sell all of our equipment. We would be out of business immediately and without any means of income. I now know what makes people go Postal. The panic I felt those first few moments was smothering. I looked at Brian "What are we going to do.?" And then I prayed. God had been with us all the way and we sure needed him now.

I called Mr. Knier, and he put a stop to all the threats. It sure was an unhappy day, but at least we had a little time. We set about meeting with the "credit risk manager" from Farm Credit, Farm Credit's attorney and Mr. Knier.

We had to go through paragraph by paragraph what Farm Credit wanted. First, they said we had given up all of our rights when we signed the papers back in 2001 according to the Farm Act. I asked to see the Farm Act, but it was not forth coming. Farm Credit took all of our stock, so according to them, we were no longer members and could not contact the Board of Directors or have any one else within Farm Credit take over our loan. We were not to contact anyone about our loan as we were no longer members. It certainly is a feeling of being hung out to dry.

Next, Farm Credit demanded that we sell all of the livestock by March 1, 2004. They demanded that we give them a deed in escrow to certain pieces of land. The land they wanted didn't make any sense. We sat there with two attorneys and the "credit manager" discussing us as if we weren't there. I finally got fed up with it and I said to the credit manager, "I will sell the whole farm, rather than let you have our land." This guy had grown up in our home town. We had known his family ever since we had moved over to Prescott in 1966. He wanted to make conversation, how was my sister, what were our kids doing, etc. He was turning our life upside down and he wanted to be sociable. This business was upsetting enough. I said, "Let's just get this done."

Our forbearance agreement was about forty pages long and outlined every move we could make. We were forced to agree to have an auction sale on the machinery March 15, 2004. We could not keep our cattle and finish raising the babies to slaughter weight. No matter what, we had to have Farm Credit paid off by the 1st of May, 2004, or else these deeds in escrow would become effective and Farm Credit would own the land and we would have nothing. That land is like every other farmer's–retirement money!

Like so many other farm families who find themselves in this predicament, all we are trained to do is farm. The feelings of despair weigh pretty heavy. Who do you turn to when the people that said they would help suddenly are trying to destroy everything you have worked so hard to achieve? We tried to keep our animals and we were told that if we did not agree Farm Credit could come and get them tomorrow. We'd be better off going along with what they wanted. What Brian and I want does not mean anything. So it's done, signed, and we will have to live with the agreement. Now we will have to see if anyone wants to buy part of the land.

Rumors abound. A couple of the neighbors have contacted the real estate company asking when Farm Credit is selling the land. One young man is bragging that his dad is buying our farm for him. His dad is a friend of the "credit risk manager" for Farm Credit. Everyone else seems to know more of our business than we do.

CHAPTER 33

JULY–DECEMBER 2003

As anyone knows when you start a lawsuit, it takes years to go through the court system. We filed our lawsuit against Consumers Energy in 2000 and here it is 2003. We are going to court again for a hearing in front of Judge Ronald Bergeron. This is about our third court hearing. As we started, Judge Bergeron asks why we were there. Judge Bergeron has read all the material, which he says is abundant and he had not received it only in the last few days. There were motions that were to have been made before the end of June and it is now July, so why is everything late? Mr. Reynolds says, "In Wayne County they only have to file the motions, not hear them."

Judge Bergeron says, "This is not Wayne County and we do things different in Ogemaw County and what part of the order did Mr. Reynolds not understand?" Judge Bergeron then asks our attorney David Aldrich what he understood the motion to mean.

Mr. Aldrich said "I understood that the motions had to be heard before the end of June and that I told Mr. Reynolds that same thing." Mr. Reynolds agreed that he had been told. Judge Bergeron finally said he would hear the arguments today, but that Consumers had to agree not to bring any sanctions against us in the future.

Mr. Reynolds then went on to present his case. That Brian had gone to a meeting and received material on "stray voltage". We had subscribed to the Hoard's Dairyman that had articles published on "stray voltage", and electricity and "stray voltage" and any other electrical phenomenon were all under the same umbrella of electricity." He went on and on about how we could have known, should have known all about electricity.

"If you have cows and you have electricity, you have to know that sooner or later you will have trouble." He then brought up the portalogger that was on our farm taking voltage measurements. How the first graph proved that we knew we had electrical problems before we claimed we did since that first graph was done in May of 1998, although we said we did not start to think we had a problem until December of 1998. I wanted to jump up and down. That graph was not from our farm, but was part of the tutorial for the portalogger program to explain how the graphs would look and what information was on each graph. We had told Consumers about this in the interrogatories almost two years ago.

Finally, after about one and one half hours, it's Mr. Aldrich's turn. He explains that this is not a typical "stray voltage" case; it never has been. It is a power quality case where the sags, swells, harmonics and transients cause the cows to not produce and to get shocks. For all the information that Mr. Reynolds claims Consumers sent to us, nowhere in the literature does it describe harmonics or transients, or how they affect farms. Judge Bergeron has an engineering degree, so he can understand the arguments better than most people.

It is getting close to noon and Judge Bergeron wants to know how much longer Mr. Reynolds is going to be with his arguments. Mr. Reynolds says he hasn't gotten started on the fraud charges, and he'd like to come back after lunch. Judge Bergeron says he has a full afternoon case load. Mr. Reynolds says it will take him about half an hour to cover the fraud charges. Judge Bergeron asks Mr. Aldrich how long it will take him and he replies half as long as Mr. Reynolds. Mr. Reynolds starts his dialog. When he finishes, Judge Bergeron told him that took him seventeen minutes. Mr. Aldrich stood true to his word and took about half that time.

Judge Bergeron asks Mr. Reynolds who James Schrandt is and what does he do for Consumers Company? Mr. Reynolds says he is an engineer and works in the Agriculture Division of Consumers. Mr. Schrandt had written us a letter on how the levels of harmonics were within their limits. The letter was part of the material that Judge Bergeron had looked at for the proceedings. Judge Bergeron wanted to know where in Consumers literature it described harmonics or transients. Mr. Reynolds admitted "Nowhere." Judge Bergeron ruled that he should let us go to the jury on just the letter that Mr. Schrandt had written, but he felt we had proven our case and would allow it to continue with a jury trial.

At that point the attorneys discussed how long each attorney would to need to plead his case. Mr. Aldrich said it would take him about a week, and Mr. Reynolds said it would take him about three weeks. Judge Bergeron said that after a week, he could not guarantee uninterrupted time because the criminals in Ogemaw County kept the courts pretty busy. Mr. Aldrich volunteered to help Mr. Reynolds make up a book for each of the jury persons. Then the discussion went to how long it took Mr. Reynolds to get to the point and that the jury might need something to keep them going and Mr. Aldrich said that they could give the jury a jar of pickles. That started Mr. Reynolds on a tirade that he hated pickles and how useless pickles were. Judge Bergeron leaned forward and quietly said, "I like pickles, and I come from a county that raises pickles." Mr. Reynolds couldn't get his foot out of his mouth fast enough. I loved Judge Bergeron's sense of humor.

At one of the other court dates, after Consumers had appealed Judge Bergeron's ruling to keep the court proceedings in Circuit Court instead of letting them go before the Public Service Commission, Judge Bergeron said to Mr. Reynolds, "If the Appellant Court thinks I'm such a bad judge, they will rule against me."

Mr. Reynolds back pedaled and said "Well Your Honor we're not insinuating that you're a bad judge." At least now we have a court date.

August of 2003 brought a major black out across the Midwest and east coast. We were not without electricity, but the systems we have in place on our farm picked up the exact minute the electricity went off. If we could monitor an event like that, don't tell me the events we measured on our farm weren't real. For whatever reason, we can pick up events that happen on our substation, and I know that they correlated with the things that happened to our cows. If only I could make other people understand the same things. As I have said to Consumers, "The experts will cross each other out, but the jury will be able to see the difference on each graph and see what is going on at our farm."

I have talked to some of the legislators we have been working with trying to get them to see what an antiquated grid our national system is and needs to be upgraded. They all comment that when the lights went out, they thought about us. Well, that is good, but I hope somewhere in all of the policies on energy we do in the future, they will put something in place to correct the issues. Our electrical shortage is not going to get better on its own. Like so many of the things that we have taken for granted, it all needs to be upgraded. We demand so much from systems that were not intended to have this much pressure placed on them. We have increased our usage above and beyond anyone's wildest dreams.

So many people don't know the history of electricity, and it is important to know how it was invented, the arguments that went along with the decisions on whether it should be AC or DC.

When Thomas Edison invented electricity, he understood the possibilities of issues with electricity and provided for it. In his patent papers it is written, "All of such conductors from the generators at the station to the lamps are made in pairs—one for the out going current and the other for the returning current of electricity, the circuits throughout the system being complete or round metallic, the conductors of which are well insulated from each other and from the earth. The use of the earth for one-half of the circuit would largely increase the difficulties arising from the grounding of the conductors or the crossing of the conductors among themselves or with the conductors of other circuits to such an extent that a system so constructed would be impracticable." Isn't it funny that the man who invented electricity should warn about using the earth to return electricity?

In 1900 Thomas Edison and Nicola Tesla debated which was better, AC, Alternating current, or DC, Direct current power, for generating electricity.

Nicola Tesla: "Alternating Current will allow the transmission of electrical power to any point on the planet, either through wires or through the air, as I have demonstrated."

Thomas Edison: "Transmission of AC over long distances requires lethally high voltages and should be outlawed. To allow Tesla and Westinghouse to proceed with their proposals is to risk untold deaths by electricide."

Tesla: "How will DC power a 1,000 horsepower electric motor as well as a single light bulb? With AC the largest as well as the smallest load may be driven from the same line."

Edison: "The most efficient and proper electrical supply for every type of device from the light bulb to the phonograph is Direct Current at low voltage."

Tesla: "A few large AC generating plants, such as my hydro-electric station at Niagara Falls, are all you need: from these, power can be distributed easily wherever it is required."

Edison: "Small DC generating plants, as many as are required, should be built according to local needs, after the model of my power station in New York City."

Early AC dominance: After Edison introduced his DC power stations; the first of their kind in the world, the demand for electricity became overwhelming. Soon, the need to send power over long distances in rural and suburban America was paramount. How did the two power systems compare in meeting this need?

AC—Alternating current could be carried over long distances via a relatively small line given an extremely high transmission voltage of 50,000 volts or above. The high voltage could then be transformed down to lower levels for residential, office and industrial use.

DC—While higher in quality and more efficient than alternating current, DC power could not be transformed or transmitted over distances via small cables without suffering significant losses through resistance.

The Result: AC power became the standard of all public utilities, overshadowing issues of safety and efficiency and forcing manufacturers to produce appliances and motors compatible with the national grid.

The 100 YEAR OLD POWER SCHEME: With AC power the only option available from power utilities, the world came to rely

AC DEVICES—1950	DC DEVICES—2000
Electric Typewriters	Computers, Printers, CRT's, Scanners
Adding Machines	CD-ROMs, Photocopiers
Wired, Rotary Telephones	Wired, Cordless & Touch Tone Phones
Teleprinter	Answering Machines, Modems, Faxes, Videoconferencing, Internet, Intranet
Early Fluorescent Lighting	Advanced Fluorescent Lighting with Electronic Ballast, Gas Discharge Lighting
Radios, Early TV's	HDTV's, CD Players, Video-cassette Recorders
Record Players	Cable & Satellite Decoders, Game Consoles
Electric Range	Microwave Ovens
Fans, Furnaces	Electronically Controlled HVAC Systems

almost exclusively on AC-based motors and other appliances, and the efficiencies and disadvantages of AC power became accepted as unavoidable.

Nicola Tesla's development of the polyphase induction AC motor was a key step in the evolution of AC power applications. His discoveries contributed greatly to the development of dynamos, vacuum bulbs and transformers, strengthening the existing AC power scheme of 100 years ago. Compared to DC and Edison's finding, AC power is inefficient because of the energy lost with the rapid reversals of the current's polarity. We often hear these reversals as the familiar sixty cycles per second (60hertz) hum of the appliance. AC power is also prone to harmonic distortion, which occurs when there is a disruption in the ideal AC sinusoidal power wave shape. Since most of today's technological advances of on-site power devices are DC, there is a need to use inverters to produce AC through the system and then back to DC into the end source of power. These inverters are inefficient: energy is lost as much as up to fifty percent when these devices are used. This characteristic is evident in many of today's electronic devices that have internal converters, such as fluorescent lighting.

AC/DC: 1950 to 2000 the discovery of semiconductors and the invention of the transistor, along with the growth of the American economy, triggered a quiet but profound revolution in how we use electricity. Changes over the last half-century have brought the world into the era of electronics with more and more machines and appliances operating internally on DC power and requiring more and more expensive solutions for the conversion and regulation of incoming AC supply.

A WORLD OUT of PHASE

Over the last fifty years, we have moved steadily from an electro-mechanical to an electronic world—a world where most of our electrical devices are driven by Direct Current, and where most of our non-fossil fuel energy sources, such as photovoltaic cell and batteries, deliver their power as a DC supply.

THE PROBLEM: Despite these changes, the majority of today's electricity is still generated, transported and delivered as Alternating Current. Converting AC to DC and integrating alternative DC sources with the mainstream AC supply are inefficient and expensive activities that add significantly to capital costs and lock us all into archaic and uncompetitive utility pricing structures.

THE SOLUTION: Nextek's AC/DC integration technology represents a breakthrough in on-site electrical management, combining the availability of AC power with the quality and efficiency of a DC supply.

NEXTEK BENEFITS: •Easy conversion of AC lighting fixtures to DC-powered units.

•Easy conversion of AC grid power into DC power into lighting systems.

•Highly efficient management of peak loads.

•Complete continuity of supply through the seamless integration of rechargeable batteries.

•Complete continuity of alternative energy sources such as PV, micro turbines and fuel cells.

•Future-proof lighting and other systems to be developed.

•A world which Thomas Edison envisioned which is clean, efficient and less costly.

THE CYCLE of 100 YEARS NEEDS to be ADDRESSED for a SUSTAINABLE POWER FUTURE

• The computer industry alone accounts for fifteen percent of the total power in America.

• Fossil Fuel needs need to be slowed to prevent global warming concerns.

• On-site power using DC to the end-source is the most efficient use of power.

• No conversion losses using DC power for the full potential of alternative energy.

So the debate on the effects of electricity has been an ongoing issue for the last hundred years. You can see how slanted the utility companies' view is and how hard it is fight the battle with them. Maybe in the next hundred years things will change, but the utility companies certainly are not going to willingly change as long as farmers go out of business and go away and they have the ability to make legislators and judges believe them over the people that have to live in these situations. For us, we march on toward a trial date of January of 2004. If we can present our case before a jury, we might be able to get Consumers to upgrade their lines in our area.

Consumers is running true to form. We believed we would have a court date in January; Consumers has appealed Judge Bergeron's decision to allow us to go to a jury. It could take up to two years before the Appeals Court decide if they will hear our case. So many cases like this have to go through all of these hoops.

I receive a call from a girl named Rachel Fiechter. She used to work with my son-in-law Brian who lives in Arlington, Virginia. They met for lunch one day and she told him she needed a project for her film production class and she asked him if he knew of anything she could report on and he said "Do I have a story for you!" Rachel and I talked and I briefly tell her about the electricity and what had happened on our farm. She decides that she would like to come out and interview us. She and Shawn, her camera man, come to spend a few days with us. We show her our facilities and spend some time answering questions, and then we go on a tour around our area and to Michigan State, meet with David Aldrich, our attorney. They only can stay a couple of days. But they found out the story was a lot bigger than they ever thought it would become. I told them it was just the tip of the iceberg. I gave them a list of names of people to talk to like Dave Stetzer and Dr. Graham. The film they want to do will be a documentary to be placed into film festivals.

Our property has not sold; we have talked to another bank. We need to sell some of the land to bring debt down. If we can do that, the bank says to call them and they will see what they can do. Farm Credit has not been the best to work with; they appear to be using us as an open check book. Every time the "credit risk manager" wants to talk to their attorney, it is charged to us. We still have not been able to get a copy of the Farm Act that they say holds the key as to why they think we gave up our rights. As the year comes to a close, we are no closer to a resolution than before.

Chapter 34

January–June 2004

We go to Lansing in the middle of January to testify on a hearing for Consumers reliability of electricity. The utilities will have to repair their lines in a very short time after an outage. I tell them about the problems we have had in our area. Finally, last summer the tree that has been on our lines fell down enough to almost break the distribution line down the road from our house. Consumers' local guys came out and apologized for not taking care of it sooner, but no one had told them there was a problem. I showed the Judge the branch that had three marks on it where the hot lines had actually burned three lines in the branch. It was like preaching to the choir because who should be the Judge at the Public Service hearing but no other than Judge Nickerson. It seems like he should know by now! It sure does tick off the men representing Consumers that we keep coming back.

Time is running out for us on the farm. We are going to set up an auction sale for the land. It will be held on February 28 and the machinery sale will be held on March 5. We hope we can sell enough land to pay off Farm Credit and still be able to keep some of the land and continue to farm.

The "credit risk manager" can't believe we're going to auction the land. What did he think! I told him last June that I'd sell every acre before I'd let them have it! The wheels of motion have started and there is no stopping it now. Brian is working on the equipment to get it ready for the sale.

I don't know how to help him; the cows were mine, and I'm the one who milked them. Brian raised the feed and fed them, but the land and the machinery were his babies.

This is so hard for him. When we sold the cows, at least we had the land and the machinery to keep us busy and enable us to go on with our life. Even though it had been really hard to switch what we always thought we'd be doing for the rest of our lives milking cows. Now our future is once again up in the air.

I found out just how much stress Brian was under when he came home one night from a meeting and went to the tool shed to put another coat of paint on the tractor that my oldest daughter always said was hers. He came to the house about 11:30 p.m. and told me we needed to go to the hospital. He has had an irregular heart beat that had been controlled with medicine until a year or so before when they had done a procedure to eliminate the circuit causing the problems. This was not supposed to happen again. He has to have an echogram done on his heart. No problems are found, which is good, but it takes about three days in the hospital to correct the irregular heart beat and get him back home. This worries me a lot. I don't know how he is going to react to the actual sale.

The day of the land sale dawns. My oldest daughter comes home to be with us, but the other kids are so far away. They call and offer support, but there is nothing any of them can do for us. The sale is being held at our local township hall. A lot of people have come. Some are close by while others are from down state. The land has been split into about thirty parcels. The bidding will consist of putting parcels together. It is really complicated and takes a computer to keep track of what is happening. Some of the people who are watching the sale say a group has gotten together trying to get the land for $500 per acre and are not bidding each other up. That seemed to work for a while, then someone split the group up and they had to put land back together again, but the price went up.

Finally, it is all over. I don't know how we made out yet. Monday we have to go down to the attorney and pick what we will let go. This is a tough weekend!

When we get home around 4:00 p.m., I look out my kitchen window, I can see all the way to the back of our property, and I can see the neighbor kids riding their snowmobiles across the back fields. Their uncle has the bid on those fields and I guess they are laying claim to them already! Anyone who was intending on buying land had to have a certified check from the Bank. Some of them told the teller that they were going to a government sale, thinking that Farm Credit was in charge of the sale and they were

going to get a deal. I don't know if we can keep any of the land
or not. There is a bid on our tri-level, 3600 square foot house and
120 acres for $60,000.

We haven't slept very well this weekend; we just don't know
what to do! I have prayed a lot for guidance. I got up around 4:00
a.m., pushed a pencil and came up with an idea. As we are on our
way down to the Attorney in Bay City, I place a call to the Banker
I had talked to last fall. I told him we were going to have to let all
the land go in order to clear Farm Credit unless he could loan us
enough money to take them out of the picture. Then we could
keep the heart of the farm. He placed his faith in us and agreed to
give us the money we would need.

We met and went through the land and marked what land we
would let go and what land we were keeping. Farm Credit was not
too happy with us; we'd managed to keep our farm together. But
the cost was horrific! It cost us $ 6,000 for our own attorney and
$30,000 for Farm Credit's attorney. They charged for every phone
call that the credit risk manager made to their attorney. There
were more calls made than days in the year at that point.

We had to pay for the call that the Board of Directors made to
their attorney when they found out that they could not take all of
our stock away from us. According to the Farm Act of 1976, Farm
Credit did not have the right to take away all of our stock. Farm
Credit gave us back one share two weeks before we paid them off.
The Farm Act that the "credit risk manager" had crammed down
our throat since 2000. There were a lot of things that Farm Credit
had done that were not allowed in the Farm Act. We had called
our US representative Debbie Stabenow's office. She had written
a letter to the Federal Credit Administration. They control the
money Farm Credit receives. Representative Stabenow has asked
them to investigate our situation. I hope they will not do this to
someone else, but since no one in Farm Credit seems to have
control over the "credit risk manager," he will do the same thing
to someone else. There are humane ways to work with farmers
when they run into a problem, but what was done to us was a long
way from humane treatment; the threats, the abuse of our money
as in calling the attorney so much when everything was laid out
in the forbearance agreement we had been forced to sign, and,

finally, the runaround when the check for the machinery was made out and we had to sign it.

Instead of having the check at the Farm Credit office, they had it at the attorney's office. But when we got there, they did not know where the check was. The attorney was out of the office even though he knew we were coming. We had to go to our attorney's office. Then they found the check, so we had to go back. Another attorney had to watch us sign the check. And it cost us $60.00 to sign our names. From talking to other people who have run into the same problems, Farm Credit has never been very helpful. No one deserves this kind of treatment.

This is all we know how to do and we are not ready to let it go!

The reality is there is nothing we can do to save all that we have put together. We finally got a copy of the Farm Act that Farm Credit has been talking about since 2000; our attorney Henry Knier got it for us. That is when we found out Farm Credit did not have the right to take all of our stock. I wrote a letter to each of the Board of Directors of Farm Credit outlining what had happened to us, and I said to them "As you set at the Board table, look to the left and look to the right and know that if this can happen to us with seventy percent equity, it can happen to each of you!"

After the land sale, we had a few days to sell all of the cattle. We had worked so hard to get the barns back full again and have just now gotten to where we have all the pens full. We still have half a silo full of feed that will stay there. We have to get all the barns cleaned out because the machinery sale is this weekend. Brian's brothers and his nephew help get the machinery placed and the shop and shed cleaned out with all the stuff to be auctioned. The kids come from Washington, DC, to film our sale and talk to some of the people in the area who have had problems with Consumers. This is so hard!

On the day of the auction there are about 500 people here! I go out to the sale, but I can't take this. I know it is not anyone's fault, but I feel like a rabbit being hunted by the foxes. Some friends we haven't seen in twenty years come up to see us and offer moral support, as does one of my cousins. Some of our kids are here! This means more to us than we can ever say! I will never go to another auction sale without feeling vulnerable, hurt, scared, let down, angry, and so many more indescribable emotions. I will never be happy going to a sale of any kind. A person's whole life is open for everyone to see and the wound runs very deep, especially when this is a sale that you are not ready to have. We were not ready to quit and retire somewhere!

Rachel and Shawn were at our house taking pictures of all the things going on, and talking to all of these people. Shawn followed us around, camera in tow. One of the places we went was out in the free stall barn; he wanted to film me looking at the empty barn. As I stood there while he was filming, I remembered what it was like when times were good and the cows enjoyed the barn. Then I thought about an advertisement where the Indian stood looking at the burned forest with tears running down his face, regret for what man had done to destroy his forest. I know tears were on my face and I felt the same feelings as I saw what had been done to my barn that had been so alive with cows, now standing desolate and gone forever!

Thank God, it is over! Several years ago, I sat in church one Sunday when we had a guest speaker. He told us about his mother, a lady from our congregation who had died the same time as my dad. He said he had a time when he had some bills to pay and did not know where the money was going to come from. His mother told him to place it in God's hand and everything would be all right. He said he prayed about it and placed it in God's hands. A few days later some unexpected money came to him, enough to pay the bills he needed to pay. That really hit me! I had been a Christian since I was twelve years old. I had prayed about a lot of things, each time I took a test in school, but I never had placed my whole being into God's hands. I decided to do that. It takes a lot of prayer and it is really the hardest thing to do because we always want to be in control. But when I leave things in God's hands, I can sleep at night and don't have a stomachache. But it is a challenge to be able to leave everything to God. He has been good to us. We would not be where we are without His guidance.

Farm Credit had not been good to us. They had agreed to help us when we wanted to sell the cows. They had said they would work with us to be able to keep our farm going. They lied to us about the Farm Act and what was in it. For all the years we had devoted to them they were sure quick to turn their back on us. All the money we invested in them over the years—we always paid our way—never received a buy down as some did. But I'm glad we are done with them and can move on to a better future.

The month of May brings us to a hearing at the Court of Appeals. This is what we have waited for such a long time. Consumers Energy had appealed Judge Bergeron's decision to allow us to go to a jury trial back in July of 2003. This court appearance will determine legally how we proceed with our case. Rachel and Shawn want to come and film the proceedings. David Aldrich gives Rachel the names of whom she needs to contact. He tells me they never allow filming of these proceedings, and all three Judges have to agree. He was absolutely floored when the Judges agreed to the filming.

We meet Rachel and Shawn at the Court House in Pellston. The Judges are William Whitbeck, Richard Griffin and J. Borrello. We go into the Court room early and listened to several cases in the morning. Mr. Reynolds, the Consumers attorney, came in and Mr. Aldrich says to Mr. Reynolds, "That the proceedings were going to be filmed by Rachel and Shawn."

Mr. Reynolds says "I wish I would have known that they were going to film today, cameras always make you look heavy."

Mr. James Brenner and another man came for Consumers' side. When it came time for our case, the court took a recess so that Rachel and Shawn could get their equipment set up. The Court gave a lot of lenience letting them in to the court room. I'm not sure Consumers liked it.

Mr. Reynolds argued his case. At one point he said that in 1994 Brian attended the seminar and that Consumers came out to test for "stray voltage". And that at that point we should have known we had a "stray voltage" problem.

Judge Borrello asked him if he was saying we had "stray voltage".

Mr. Reynolds replied, "Well, your Honor, I wouldn't say that. I'm saying that they could have hired an expert to do testing."

Judge Borrello says, "You are the experts, aren't you? Just when do they get to sue you?"

Then Mr. Reynolds laid into Mr. Aldrich, about a case (Benn) at the Court of Appeals he had lost. Mr. Aldrich said, "For that reason alone the Court should know I would not bring a 'stray voltage' case before them. This was and had always been a different case, for poor power quality, not stray voltage."

Soon the arguments were over and our case rested in the hands of the Court. As we left the court room the Consumers men, Brenner and someone else were having a heated discussion with Mr. Reynolds. Rachel asked to speak with them, but they turned away. Rachel asked me what I thought, and I told her it was in God's hands now! Now we wait!

A couple of weeks later we went to the Consumers annual meeting. As usual I had the same question to ask, "When are you going to upgrade the distribution lines in front of my house?" Apparently I ticked off the CEO because for the first time in four years he said we had been to the Court of Appeals and they had ruled in Consumers favor. I replied that the Court had not made a decision yet, and I would keep coming back until we got a resolution to the issue. That was the first time they had ever mentioned we had sued them. I apparently make them uncomfortable.

Chapter 35

July–December 2004

In August of 2004 we received a ruling, not in our favor. Judges Whitbeck and Griffin were both up for reelection. It read in part:

The applicable limitations period for plaintiffs" (us) negligence claim is three years. However, where the discovery rule applies, a claim does not accrue for purposes of the limitations period until a plaintiff discovers, or with the exercise of reasonable diligence should have discovered, (1) an injury and (2) the casual connection between a defendant's breach of duty and the injury.

Although plaintiffs might not have understood with any degree of specificity the technical aspects of stray voltage, the evidence reveals that they did know, or should have known, that electricity supplied by defendant was potentially harming their animals and, in turn, causing their production to suffer.

Accordingly, we conclude that, for purposes of the discovery rule, it is sufficient to start the limitations period for a negligence claim based on problems with electricity supplied by a defendant that a plaintiff owner or operator of a livestock operation has a particular reason to believe that problems with electricity supplied by the defendant are harming the plaintiff's livestock. Critically, as applied to this case, this means that whatever differences there are between "stray voltage" and "poor power quality," they are immaterial to the determination of when the limitations period began to run because the discovery rule would be satisfied by plaintiffs having knowledge from which they should have identified defendant's electricity may have done so.

Indeed, it is reasonable to presume that an investigation of potential harm from defendant's electricity triggered by "stray voltage" concerns should also have uncovered any "poor power quality" problems, so that information suggesting a significant potential for concern about the former problem would provide sufficient notice to plaintiffs of poor power quality problem for purposes of triggering the discovery rule. Defendant presented uncontradicted evidence that plaintiff Brian Bellville attended a seminar in 1994, considerably more than three years before the filing of plaintiffs' complaint in 2001, and expressed a concern about stray voltage on plaintiffs' farm from defendant's electricity at that point.

Importantly, this Court noted "that Michigan courts have not recognized a cause of action for continuing negligence. This rejection of a cause of action for "continuing negligence" can only be understood to mean that a failure to correct a negligently created condition that has already started to cause recurring problems for a particular plaintiff cannot be considered to involve independent tortuous acts so as to provide a separate basis for a negligence claim by the plaintiff or to support application of the continuing wrongful acts doctrine. Thus, plaintiffs' allegations related to defendant failing to maintain or upgrade its equipment resulting in continuing harm to their cows does not prevent their negligence claim from being barred by the statute of limitations because undisputed evidence indicates that the alleged problems began more than three years before the filing of their complaint. Because of this, plaintiffs' suggestion that they are not asserting that there was negligence when the electrical system was originally installed is immaterial.

In its brief in support of its motion for summary disposition, defendant (Consumers) specifically argued that plaintiffs (us) did not cease dairy farming after their alleged experts told them that defendant had falsely advised them regarding electrical problems at the farm, but rather continued their dairy farming for one and a half more years, which, defendant contended, belied a claim that they actually relied on any alleged misrepresentations by defendant. Thus, defendant specifically identified the issue of whether there was evidence of actual reliance by plaintiffs.

Judge Borrello did not agree with the other two Judges and he wrote in part:

Statues of limitations are legislative restrictions on the time frame within which a plaintiff may bring suit for particular claims. Generally, a claim accrues "when all the elements have occurred and can be alleged in a complaint." But our Legislature, by creating statutes of limitations, did not intend to usurp a plaintiff's right to bring a claim before the plaintiff becomes cognizant of a possible cause of action. Thus, to avoid depriving a plaintiff of the chance to pursue an otherwise valid claim "because of the latent nature of the injury or the inability to discover the causal connection between the injury and the defendant's breach of duty owed to plaintiff," we apply the discovery rule. Otherwise, we would be "declaring the bread stale before it is baked."

Here, applying the discovery rule would not degrade the policy reasons behind the stature of limitations because plaintiffs have presented evidence regarding both a "factually verifiable consequence of some action by the defendant," and "an objective external standard against which to measure the defendant's conduct." As will be discussed, plaintiffs were diligent in attempting to discover the nature of their injuries.

Defendant is not the victim of unfair delay or surprise, as it was defendant's actions that contributed to plaintiff's failure to previously bring suit. The objective and factually verifiable evidence in this case obviates a finding that plaintiffs' claims are plaintiffs' claims are fraudulent.

I would hold that where one party prevents or actively partici-pates in preventing another party from discovering the true nature of his or her injuries, as long as there is objective, veri-fiable evidence from which to assess the claim, the discovery rule should apply. As such, I would hold that the common-law discovery rule applies to the case at hand.

I would next analyze whether plaintiffs (us) in this case, despite the expiration of the statute of limitations, are nonetheless protected by the discovery rule. The majority relies on Jackson Co Hog Producers to hold that, assuming the discovery rule applies, the statute of limitations did not toll during the period of time when defendant (Consumers) in this case insisted that problems with plaintiffs'(us) cattle were not the result of an irregular power flow for which defendant (Consumers) was responsible. But there is a critical distinction between Jackson Co hog Producers and this case: there, the defendant (Consumers) did not test for electrical problems or represent to the plaintiffs that no electrical problems existed. Here, though, both those things occurred: plaintiffs (us) requested and obtained defendant's (Consumers) expert opinion regarding the potential electrical problems on plaintiffs' farm, and defendant (Consumers) explicitly denied any culpability.

I do not agree with the majority that the difference between stray voltage and other electrical problems is "immaterial to the determination of when the limitations period began to run—." Defendant (Consumers) claims that it tested only for stray voltage, so it did not misrepresent that there was no stray voltage on plaintiffs' farm. "Plaintiffs" (us) expert eventually found that there were a variety of electrical problems on plaintiffs' (us) farm.) Yet defendant (Consumers) also argues that plaintiffs (us) cannot claim that they should not have suspected other electrical problems because "stray voltage" is actually a generic term encompassing many types of electrical problems.

To dispose of this claim, it is only logical that one or the other of defendant's assertions must be accepted as to both the statute of limitations matter and the fraudulent concealment claim. If stray voltage is the generic term defendant asserts that it is, then plaintiffs (us) presented a genuine issue of material fact that defendant (Consumers) fraudulently concealed the existence of electrical problems on plaintiffs'(us) farm. But if stray voltage is but one type of electrical problem, and defendant (Consumers) tested only for the specific problem of stray voltage, then I cannot find that plaintiffs (had an "actual concern" about other electrical problems in 1994 when they specifically expressed concern about "stray voltage.

I fully agree that at the time when a plaintiff knows, or with due diligence, should know that the plaintiff has a potential cause of action; the stature of limitations must begin to run. But the key in this case is the test used to determine whether a plaintiff knew or should have known. While that test, applied in Jackson

Co Hog Producers, dictated that the statute of limitations had expired as to the plaintiffs there, in this case, it has the opposite effect.

I do not agree with the majority that the difference between stray voltage and other electrical problems is "immaterial to the determination of when the limitations period began to run...." Bellville v Consumers Energy Co. Defendant (Consumers) claims that it tested only for stray voltage, so it did not misrepresent that there was no stray voltage on plaintiffs' (us) farm. (Plaintiffs expert eventually found that there were a variety of electrical problems on plaintiffs' farm.) Yet defendant (Consumers) also argues that plaintiffs (us) cannot claim that they should not have suspected other electrical problems because "stray voltage" is actually a generic term encompassing many types of electrical problems.

To dispose of this claim, it is only logical that one or the other of defendant's assertions must be accepted as to both the statute of limitations matter and the fraudulent concealment claim. If stray voltage is the generic term defendant (Consumers) asserts that it is, then plaintiffs (us) presented a genuine issue of material fact that defendant (Consumers) fraudulently concealed the existence of electrical problems on plaintiffs' farm. But if stray voltage is but one type of electrical problem, and defendant (Consumers) tested only for the specific problem of stray voltage, then I cannot find that plaintiffs (us) had an "actual concern" about other electrical problems in 1994 when they specifically expressed concern about "stray voltage".

In Jackson Co Hog Producers, this Court analyzed whether the plaintiffs (Jackson) were entitled to bring a cause of action after the statute of limitations expired where the plaintiffs (Jackson) experienced ramifications of stray voltage on their cattle for more than three years before filing suit in October, 1993. Id. at 78–81.

The defendant submitted the testimony of several of the plaintiffs (Jackson) employees who stated that they suspected a stray voltage problem at the farm before May, 1988, and that they had taken steps to alleviate the problem such as attempting to

ground the electricity. Id. At 79. The Court also considered that
the defendant had periodically mailed brochures about stray
voltage to the plaintiffs' (Jackson) facilities. ID. The plaintiff's
(Jackson) denied suspecting a stray voltage problem, claiming
that the employees' testimony was misconstrued. Id.At 80.

This Court assumed that the discovery rule applied and
correctly noted that under that rule, a cause of action does not
accrue until "a plaintiff discovers, or through the exercise of
reasonable diligence should have discovered (1) an injury and
(2) the causal connection between the injury and a defendant's
breach of duty." Id. At 78, citing Lemmerman, supra at 66.
Importantly, this Court recognized that determining whether a
cause of action has accrued is an objective test, "based on
objective facts, and not on what a particular plaintiff subjec-
tively believed." Jackson Co Hog Producers, supra at 78. This
Court then reasoned as follows:

[Plaintiffs were aware, or at least should have been aware, that
they were suffering damages as a result of stray voltage.
Although plaintiffs might not have understood with any degree
of specificity the technical aspects of stray voltage, the
evidence reveals that they did know, or should have known,
that electricity supplied by defendant was potentially harming
their animals and, in turn, causing their production to suffer.
Further, even if plaintiffs believed that the steps that they had
taken to alleviate the problem were successful, the continued
production problems should have alerted plaintiffs to the possibility that the electrical problem was not entirely corrected.
Accordingly, the trial court did not err in concluding that sometime before October, 1990, plaintiffs knew or should have
known, that stray voltage was causing them injury. Id. At
80–81.]

Although the facts here are strikingly similar, the resemblance
ends at the measures the current plaintiffs (us) employed to
determine the cause of their ailing cattle. In my opinion, this
factual difference renders our holding in Jackson Co Hog
Producers inapplicable to the case at hand. In the present case,
plaintiffs (us) actively attempted to discover the nature of their
cattle's injuries by summoning defendant (Consumers) to

conduct testing on their farm, but defendant (Consumers), at each testing, consistently denied any problems with the electricity supply. Defendant (Consumers) first visited plaintiffs' (us) farm in February 1994, after plaintiffs (us) requested testing, and reported were being systematically alleviated by defendant (Consumers) itself that no electrical problems existed. Although plaintiffs admittedly had concerns about stray voltage and wondered if the problems they were experiencing were electricity-related, they had no objective evidence implicating defendant, predominantly because defendant (Consumers), the expert in the field, represented conclusively that there were no electricity problems. In fact, defendant (Consumers) tested again for electrical problems in 1996,1997,and 1998, and each time, defendant (Consumers) informed plaintiffs (us) that all measurements were within normal limits and that there were no stray voltage problems at the farm. Thus, unlike the plaintiffs in Jackson Co Hog Producers, these plaintiffs (us) ongoing concerns about their cattle's health problems were being systematically alleviated by defendant (Consumers) itself.

We are required to view all evidence in the light most favorable to the nonmoving party. In that light, I would conclude as follows. At all times previous to plaintiffs (us) hiring an independent agency to test for electrical problems in 1998, only isolated questions existed, questions that as likely could have been attributed to general health issues that arise with dairy cattle under normal circumstances. In other words, the evidence demonstrates that early on in plaintiffs (us) quest to determine what was wrong with their cattle, they had no definitive, objective evidence that defendant's (Consumers) electricity was the culprit: rather, the problems they were experiencing could have just as easily been unrelated to electricity. In fact, plaintiffs (us) position had objective evidence regarding defendant's (Consumers) potential culpability, I would find that based on defendant's (Consumers) continual denials that its electrical supply or equipment was the source of plaintiffs' problems, the statute of limitations tolled until plaintiffs had objective evidence that would support a cause of action. I fail to see how we can hold a plaintiff to standard by which if the plaintiff has a completely unsubstantiated suspicion that is consistently assuaged by the party suspected of wrongdoing, the plaintiff should be required to file suit anyway. Requiring a plaintiff to file suit under these circumstances not only encourages a multitude of potentially frivolous lawsuits, but also encourages attorneys to violate MCR 2.114(D)(2) (an attorney signing a pleading certifies that "to the best of his or her knowledge, information, and belief formed after reasonable inquiry, the document is well-grounded in fact..."), and MRPC 3.1 ("A lawyer should not bring or defend a proceeding, or assert or controvert an issue therein, unless there is a basis for doing so that is not frivolous...")

The majority's result has far-reaching consequences—consequences that I strongly feel are contrary to precedent and legislative intent. The rule promulgated by the majority today gives defendant and similarly situated companies free license to inform a customer that the company is not the source of the problems the customers is experiencing, while the statute of limitations goes stampeding by. While we are traditionally concerned with preventing the opening of the so-called "floodgates of litigation," see, e.g., Campbell v Sullins, 257 Mich App 179, 189; 667 NW2d 887 (2003), Great Lakes Heating, Cooling, Refrigeration & Sheet Metal Corp v Troy School Dist, 197 Mich App 312,315,494 NW2d 863 (1992), and Randall v Delta Charter Township, 121 Mich App 26,32,328 NW2d 562 (1982), here the majority encourages it. Now, a plaintiff must—in the face of objective evidence to the contrary—file suit merely on the basis of his or her subjective belief or suspicion that a particular defendant could possibly be the cause of the damage the plaintiff is sustaining.

Now, if a plaintiff—reasonably believing that he or she has no valid claim—logically chooses not to file suit, he or she is then robbed of recourse. I cannot accept that a claim accrues when the plaintiff knows of a potential cause of action, because the word "potential" has a subjective base and is therefore as expansive as the majority's holding purports. Clearly, a plaintiff must exercise due diligence to discover whether a claim exists, as plaintiffs did here. But the majority's holding permits suit when the plaintiff's belief that a particular party is responsible for an injury is based on mere suspicion and requires suit where the plaintiff's diligent inquiry has uncovered nothing to support a valid claim.

Thus, by precluding the wronged plaintiff from bringing a claim, the majority rewards a defendant for misrepresenting facts, regardless whether the representations were intentionally made.

Moreover, plaintiffs' (us) fraudulent concealment claim is an alternative basis relief in that it provides grounds for applying the statutory discovery rule found in MCL 600.5855: If a person who is or may be liable for any claim fraudulently conceals the existence of the claim or the identity of any person who is liable for the claim from the knowledge of the person entitled to sue on a claim, the action may be commenced at any time within 2 years after the person who is entitled to bring the action discovers, or should have discovered, the existence of the claim or the identity of the person who is liable for the claim, although the action would otherwise be barred by the period of limitations.

The majority concludes that plaintiffs (us) presented no genuine issue of material fact regarding fraudulent conceal-ment, reasoning that because plaintiffs (us) failed to conduct outside testing, they cannot show that they relied on defen-dant's (Consumers) statements. I find the reverse to be true. Plaintiff's choice not to conduct outside testing inarguably demonstrates that they did rely on defendant's assertions. At the very least, the fact that we disagree on this issue demon-strates the existence of a material fact. Lytle v Malady, 458 Mich 153,191 n 3; 579 NW2d 906 (1998) (Cavanaugh J. dissenting).

Further, plaintiffs (us) abstained from filing suit against defen-dant (Consumers) after defendant repeatedly assured them that electricity was not the cause of their problems. I find that fact to be an undeniably obvious example of reliance.

And viewing the facts in the light most favorable to plaintiffs (us), plaintiffs presented a genuine issue of material fact regarding whether defendant's representations were made falsely or recklessly and with the intention that plaintiffs (us) rely on them. Campbell v Sullins, 257 Mich App 179,195:667 NW2d 887 (2003).

For the reasons stated, I would affirm the trial court's denial of defendant's motion for summary disposition.

—Stephen L Borrello

All of the legal wording is so complicated to digest. I enclosed the actual piece so you as the reader can experience the frustration to understand what is happening to the average individual in this situation. So having not been successful at the Court of Appeals, we decided to take our case to the Michigan Supreme Court for a ruling, which should take precedent over statute of limitations or the discovery rule. To say we were disappointed not to be able to take our case to a jury is an understatement. It seems Consumers certainly knows how to play the game. It's really hard to fight someone who claims they did not say or did not do anything you blame them for, and twist everything to make themselves blameless. As you can see the company put all electricity under "stray voltage" so they could start the stature of limitations running. Now we fully realized why they sent out videos and held the series of meeting offering "stray voltage" testing on farms, and as producers, we all blindly walked into these circumstances.

We, like all of the people before us, are not electrical experts. We have all done the best we could to make our farms productive, and when we ran into a problem we tried to correct it, but when it is an issue that someone else has control over, it gets to be a no win situation. That is where we find ourselves at this point in time.

As the fall comes I decide that I need to go to work. The hours are getting more difficult to fill without cattle to care for. So I go to Michigan Works. I have never had to go out and look for a job and I feel really frightened; I am not trained for an outside job. Yes, I have spent thirty years working. I have dealt with people, done all the bookkeeping, run machinery, a whole lot of different things, but am I trained in anything someone else will pay me to do?

The lady I am supposed to see isn't available today, but they show me a book that has a list of jobs. I start to cry. This is so difficult! The people are kind, but I feel so stupid, intimidated, overwhelmed. The secretary takes me in to see another lady. She closes the door, sets me down and says, "Nancy, you know you have to put this in God's hands." WOW, you talk about God's help!

I said, "I know that." We talked about what had happened to both of us. She told me she had experienced a similar life changing event. No one could have given me a better person to help me. We agreed that I would come back for some classes they offer on resumes and how to interview. I went home feeling so much better. I did put it in God's hands!

When I got home, Brian told me that his brother, Terry had said that the Turner Elevator was looking for some one to work in the office. I went right down and interviewed with Laurie Schutte who owns the elevator. She said she had some others to interview and she would get back with me.

The next day she called and I had the job! I know I can do this job. It is with farmers, and I can use the knowledge I have of farming. I'm good at bookkeeping, and I know I can learn whatever else I need to do. I'm really looking forward to this new step in my life. Since I have never worked away from home, it will be a challenge, but then I like challenges!

We have another unusual thing happen. Brian was back plowing the field that we have often wondered if there was Electro-Magnetic Fields there. It was the same field that our neighbor had chopped straw off and her cancer came back after working one week in that field. It was the same field next to the new house where the wife was diagnosed with breast cancer just about two weeks after they moved. After three or four days Brian complained of his arm hurting where he had leaned it on the arm rest in the tractor. It looked like a red circle. He went to the emergency room and they put him on antibiotics and drew a line around it. He came home and then he went fishing in Canada for the week. His arm looked good when he got home, but the next day it was swollen and red. He went back to the hospital again and this time they drained it. It had gotten infected. It took about three weeks and the highest antibiotic they could give him to get rid of it. It was chilling. It looked just like the abscesses that we had on the cows, and it had developed just as fast. Of course, no one would ever believe that the EMF fields would cause it. As Governor Granholm had said on the ditch bank a couple of years ago, "You just have to wonder!"

In December, we go to the annual Farm Bureau convention at Traverse City. At the convention the delegates vote on different resolutions that each county has passed at their annual meetings.

After their annual meetings, the passed resolutions go to the state committee and they put them all together to come up with the wording for the convention.

This year a group of us would like to get some of the wording changed in the "Stray voltage" policy that Farm Bureau has in their policy book. We'd like to add Electrical Pollution to the wording. It passed with not too much trouble. We'd like to change a little more but it takes time to change things. So many people don't understand what the issue is all about.

Farm Bureau has helped us, by submitting an amicus brief on our behalf at the Michigan Supreme Court. They are also on a committee to set up standards for "stray voltage" testing in Michigan. I just wish that this committee would have had a farmer who had experienced problems with electricity to advise them on what needs to be done. It isn't fair that the utility companies get to sway the proceedings in favor of themselves.

Another year comes to a close. Another farm in West Branch has sold their cows this year. They had sued Consumers, and settled. Consumers never fixed what needed to be done and now they have given up. It just never seems to end. As farms get bigger, they may have an advantage of getting upgraded. Consumers can upgrade under the cloak of new construction. I don't care how they do it; I just want them to do the upgrades. I only wish that everyone could have better power quality. Either Illinois or Ohio is now taking three phases to every commercial business in that state including farms. That should help tremendously; I just wish that Consumers would do the same thing in Michigan. I know by going to their annual meetings these last few years that financially Consumers is not very well off.

They got themselves in trouble a few years ago when they invested overseas. Some of those properties were sold at less than they thought they were going to make on them when they invested in them. I know it cost them on the round trip deal where they got caught trading energy on paper making it look like that division was increasing in sales. It cost the division manager her job as well as the CEO who had been there for many years. It also cost the company because they had to pay millions of dollars to get rid of these two people. The stockholders were not happy over the buy out price on the CEO and it still comes up at the annual meetings. Consumers has sold off different parts of their holdings to try and make themselves more solvent, and, as a result of these problems, perhaps they do not have the money to put into the upgrades that need to be done.

I listened to Mr. Whipple, the CEO, after Mr. McCormmick talks about integrity. After having to deal with the Company, I am not impressed! Right now I am dealing with the second CEO of Consumers since 2000. That does not speak very well for them.

CHAPTER 36

JANUARY–JUNE 2005

Our life has settled down into a routine. I go to work everyday; Brian is getting accustomed to being on his own. He is doing most of the field work by himself. It is sure different after spending thirty-nine years being together 24/7. But I love my job; it keeps me in contact with farming. We deal with mostly cash crop farmers. I never dealt with the fertilizer we put on the crops. Brian did. So making up fertilizer blends is new to me, but I really like the challenge.

We're still waiting on our case being heard at the Michigan Supreme Court. Farm Bureau has written an Amicus Brief for us. In part it reads: STATEMENT OF INTEREST OF AMICUS CURIAE AND GROUNDS SUPPORTING LEAVE TO APPEAL:

> Michigan Farm Bureau ("Farm Bureau") is the state's largest general farm organization, with over 200,000 members and associate members in sixty-seven Michigan counties, including, 47,185 farmer members. Farm Bureau's mission is to represent, protect, and enhance the business, economic, social and educational interests of its members. As the names suggests, Farm Bureau exists primarily for the advancement and improvement of the agricultural interests of Michigan and the nation.
>
> Farm Bureau has an important interest in this case because of the devastating impact that outdated and mismanaged power distribution systems have on Michigan farmers. These problems are severe, pervasive, and widespread.
>
> Farmers do not have a choice regarding where to buy electricity; they have to rely on the local electric utility. Poor power quality, "stray voltage," and other related electrical damage

affect not only dairy farms such as the appellants' (us) farm in this case, but also beef, chicken, and pork producers.

The impact of these electrical damages has been documented in Michigan since at least 1984, when three researchers examined fifty-nine Michigan dairy farms for "stray voltage" problems after numerous requests from veterinarians and farmers. The researchers found problems on thirty-two of the farms, resulting in difficulties milking the cows and "increased prevalence of clinical mastitis."

Subsequent studies have better documented the long-term effects of electrical damage on livestock. Almost all researchers agree that affected animals will begin to behave differently, avoiding certain areas where the shocks occur. Unfortunately, the places where the animals receive shocks are often feeding or water troughs, making the animals reluctant to eat or drink. This leads dairy cows to produce less or no milk, and prevents other livestock from gaining proper weight. Farmers have also reported that the problems cause birth defects, muscle spasms, sores, and can render infertile or even kill animals.

Utilities should be aware of these effects of their power distribution systems, and should be addressing them, yet more problems continue to surface everyday.

The Court of Appeals decision in this case has dealt a devastating blow to Michigan farmers whose livestock are damaged by deficient power systems: it essentially gives utilities a vested right or license to continue the wrongful failure to properly maintain their power systems which are causing harm to Michigan farms and their livestock, even if these acts still occurring and new damage has been suffered within three years before a farmer files suit.

Specifically, the Court of Appeals concluded that, if more than three years have passed since appellants could have had the merest inkling that Consumers may have been responsible for the damage appellants' (us) farm sustained, appellants are forever barred from recovering any damages even if those damages are the result of new negligence and within the applicable three-year limitation period. The Court reached this decision by rejecting the discovery rule, which is irrelevant unless the action is for damages already time-barred, and by misapplying the continuing-wrongful-acts doctrine, which is another rule that extend the time to file suit but always recognizes that wrongful acts occurring within the applicable limitation period are actionable, even if damages before then are time-barred.

The Court of Appeals here stated "that Michigan courts have not recognized a cause to recognize continuing negligence into a: … rejection of a cause of action for 'continuing negligence' [which] can only be understood to mean that a failure to correct a negligently created condition that has already started to cause recurring problems for a particular plaintiff cannot be considered to involve independent tortuous acts so as to provide a separate basis for a negligence claim by the plaintiff or to support application of the continuing wrongful acts doctrine. [Exhibit D, Court of Appeals Opinion, p3; emphasis added.] As a result, according to the Court of Appeals, Consumers need not "correct a negligently created condition that has already started to cause recurring problems "if three years have passed since the first negligent act. In others words, if appellants (us) missed the initial three-year window, Consumers has a vested right to continue its negligent conduct causing new injuries to livestock with impunity, and appellants (us) have no recourse to the law. After all, farmers cannot choose a different electric utility for their farm.

The central error of this decision is this: the Court of Appeals effectively gave Consumers a public utility license to commit torts. This is contrary to long-standing law to the contrary, such as this Court's decision in Phelps v Detroit, 120 Mich 447, 445; 79 NW 640 (1899) "… the law will not presume the continuance of a wrong, nor allow a license to continue a wrong…" (Emphasis added). If Consumers manages to get away with its negligent behavior for years—here aided by its self-help in the form of advising the farmers that it had tested for and found no stray voltage, and omitting to advise of other possible electrical damage to livestock—it is home free. And even if Consumer's legal duties are irrelevant because no one can enforce those duties. And even if Consumers breaches those duties again and again, the new acts causing damage will go unremedied as long as three years passed since the first breach. The Court of Appeals here is effectively ruling that once three years pass after the first negligent conduct, Consumers is above the law.

Remarkably, the Court of Appeals failed to recognize that its decision both encourages negligence and discourages efforts to "correct a negligently created condition." Why would a utility sustain the cost of fixing a problem if it is legally immune from any action that would require it do so? Quite simply, a utility has a lessened incentive to upgrade in rural areas where there are more livestock than humans. That is why the deficient power systems still exist; a utility lacks a proper incentive to fix them.

In this case, Consumers' failure to properly maintain its power system, now legally immunized by the Court of Appeals, resulted in the end of appellants (us) dairy farm in August 2000, within three years of filing this action. But if the Court of Appeals decision stands, appellants' (us) farm will be only one of many in Michigan that is affected. Utilities will have a disincentive to take any action whatsoever to either perform their legal duties to prevent more foreseeable harm or to correct their earlier negligence.

Most puzzling, the Court of Appeals decision is completely unjustified as a matter of law. It is not the result of the interpretation of a statute, contract, or constitutional provision, in which case the result maybe undesirable but unavoidable. This is purely a matter of law, and the public policy implications of the decision therefore can and must be considered. See, e.g., Beech Grove Investment Co v Civil Rights Comm, 380 Mich 405,430,157 NW 2 d 213 (1968) ("It is generally agreed that two of the most significant features of the common law are: (1) its capacity for growth and (2) its capacity to reflect the public policy of a given era.")

Nor is it merely an application of some long-standing common law principles. The so-called "rejection of a cause of action for continuing negligence" is extrapolated from cases that do not evidence such a rejection, and, in any case the result is patently inconsistent with this Court's body of case law stemming from

Phelps v Detroit, 120 Mich 447;79 NW 640 (1899). In light of Phelps, there is no such thing as a license to commit a tort with new tortuous acts causing new damages within the limitations period of three years before filing suit, regardless of the doctrines that may give a greater cause of action for additional damages suffered more than three years before suit, (the discovery rule and the continuing wrongs doctrine). 255

As Farm Bureau will explain further below, the cases cited by the Court of Appeals are irrelevant because this case does not involve one completed negligent act with residual, continuing damages. Consumers had not ceased to provide electricity to the Bellville farm more than three years before suit. This is a case where Consumers had never ceased its wrongful acts. As a public utility, Consumers has an affirmative duty to address foreseeable harm and especially hazard that it knows exist. Farmers have no choice regarding an electric supplier.

It defies both reason and justice that Consumers should be immune from the consequences of continuing wrongful acts, especially those within the applicable limitation period for an actionable wrong. It is also contrary to a solid body of precedent from this Court for the Court of Appeals to hold that no one may sue Consumers to end this negligent conduct or obtain any reparations, even within three years of filing suit.

In Case, supra, this Court held that a utility does not have an elevated duty of care in suits by farmers for injures to livestock. It also held that the requirements are and remain a question of fact. The Court of Appeals has effectively ruled to the contrary that there is no duty to correct the problem of inadequate and outdated power distribution systems that cause damage to livestock. The more protection that utilities receive, the less incentive they have to actually address the deficiencies of their power systems. Unless this protection is corrected, Michigan farmers will continue to suffer the consequences.

Against this backdrop, Farm Bureau asks this Court to grant leave in this case to consider both the wisdom and jurisprudence behind the Court of Appeals decision, both to correct the legal error, and for the sake of Michigan's agricultural industry.

I was most grateful for Michigan Farm Bureau supporting us at the Supreme Court, but I only wish it could have been a little sooner at the Court of Appeals. It has been a real struggle to get them to come on board. They have finally realized that with the amount of electricity that farmers are now using if the old anti-quated lines are not replaced more and more farms are going to find themselves in the same position. It has taken five long years for them to come on board, but they have started to understand the importance of the issue. If no one talks about the issue, everyone thinks it has been resolved. We are still a long ways from having it resolved, but I think each year we are making progress.

In 2000 when we went to Washington, D.C. and met with the Senators and Representatives staff members, Senator Fingold from Wisconsin had been trying for years to get the ELF system turned off, which is an underground wire to transmit communications with our submarines under the ice at the North Pole. With the Cold War no longer in existence I guess it is no longer necessary to listen to the Russians. Senator Fingold has finally been successful and they have turned it off.

It transmitted a low level voltage signal. An interesting item is that when you looked at the cancer levels in Michigan, county by county, starting at the bottom of the State and moving north, the closer you got to the ELF communication system, the higher the cancer rates. It will be interesting to look at the data after it has been turned off for a few years and see if the rates go down.

Dr. Donald Hillman has been working on the levels of electricity in his house and others around him in relation to the health issues.

They have worked with the city of Lansing and gotten some grounding done on their street, and now have filters in their houses. We put magnets in our house in various places where the electricity was a problem. That seemed to help somewhat, but we now also have filters on the circuits in our house. That seems to be working; we don't wake up in the middle of the night every night like we used to do. Some of this is trial and error on our part. There is someone out there who knows more about this, and I'm sure that the utility companies know just like they did back when it was first invented, but the dollar has always came before safety.

Sheryl Krantz, the neighbor who worked that field I have talked about that has the EMF fields in it, has died. Her cancer came back and she never could get over it. Another sad loss. Do I blame electricity? Yes! Her doctors had told her to move as she was so close to the high transmission lines. We also know that Consumers had moved her Primary neutral because she was getting shocks in her barn. Sheryl and I had talked about moving. We just did not know where else to go. How do you give up everything you have worked for all these years!

Why should we have to move when the utility companies knew from the day that electricity was invented there would be problems with it? Why should we have to disrupt our entire life for them? We and every farmer before us have dealt with the same questions. The problem is that each one has had to start from square one and learn all of the twists and turns over and over again.

Once again it is time for the annual meeting for Consumers. This year they are having it at the headquarters in Jackson. Rachel and Shawn from Washington, D.C. are going to film the proceedings off the Web cast.

Mr. Whipple and I have our usual discussion. This year I told them about the shortage of electricity we face when our Ogemaw County Fair is running. In the past the Fair has burned up transformers, and last year they put the system out three nights in a row. The whole area suffers from the lack of electricity. It's like dropping a mini city in for a week. Rose City, a small city in Ogemaw County, is now having problems with black outs. And when we have any kind of a storm, the lines go down which is a maintenance problem. Trees not trimmed often enough; for us it took three years and the tree falling down before they came to fix it. As usual, I got the standard answer. We take you seriously. We would investigate if anyone complains to us.

Those are all fine answers, but Consumers comes out to do testing between 10:00 a.m. and 2:00 p.m. when the least amount of voltage is being used, so the tests never show any problems.

I wish we could get more power to the Northern areas, our population is growing so fast and the utility companies just have not kept up. And they never get back with upgrades to the rural areas where the lines have been in place since the 1930's.

CHAPTER 37

JULY–DECEMBER 2005

M r. David Aldrich, our attorney, called to let us know that the Michigan Supreme Court has decided not to hear our case. Three Judges agreed with us, but we could not get the 4th Judge to agree.

The order from the Michigan Supreme Court reads as follows:

> On order of the Court, the Michigan Farm Bureau's motion to file a amicus curiae brief is GRANTED. The application for leave to appeal the August 24, 2004 judgment of the Court of Appeals is considered, and it is DENIED, because we are not persuaded that the questions presented should be reviewed by this Court.

Judge Cavanagh, dissents and states as follows:

> This case raises a number of significant issues, and I would grant leave to consider them. In 1994, plaintiffs (us), owners and operators of a dairy farm, were concerned about the health of their dairy herd. They requested that defendant Consumers Energy Company come to their farm and conduct testing to determine if electrical problems were negatively affecting the herd.
>
> Defendant (Consumers) conducted testing in 1994 and told plaintiffs (us) that there were no electrical problems. Defendant (Consumers) conducted subsequent testing in1997 and twice in 1998, and continued to tell plaintiffs (us) that there were no electrical problems. After plaintiffs (us) ruled out other possible causes by consulting with numerous experts about possible nutritional deficiencies and medical problems, plaintiffs (us) hired their own electrical experts in 1999 and 2000. These experts determined that defendant's (Consumers) electrical lines were the cause of the problems with the dairy herd.

Defendant (Consumers) argues that plaintiffs' claims are barred by the statute of limitations because if plaintiffs disagreed with defendant's (Consumers) assessment, plaintiffs (us) should have hired their own experts sooner. Defendant (Consumers) also does not believe that the discovery rule is applicable. In essence, defendant (Consumers) faults plaintiffs (us) for believing that defendant (Consumers) was properly conducting the testing and accurately conveying the information. But Plaintiffs (us) had no reason not to believe defendant—a company whose purpose is to provide utility service to the public—until other possible causes were subsequently eliminated. Defendant (Consumers) faults Plaintiffs (us) for not discovering that electrical that electrical problem were the source of the injuries to the herd when defendant itself was repeatedly unable to do so. However, I do not believe that it is inherently unreasonable for a customer to believe the repeated word of an electrical utility company. Therefore, whether the statute of limitations bars plaintiffs (us) claims and whether the discovery rule applies to these claims are jurisprudentially significant issues that should be addressed.

Further, I disagree that plaintiffs (us) have not established a question of material fact about whether they reasonably relied on defendant's (Consumers) alleged misrepresentations. When defendant (Consumers) repeatedly told plaintiffs (us) that electrical problems were not the cause of problems with the dairy herd, plaintiffs (us) looked to other possible causes. They did so; on the basis of the representations made by defendant (Consumers) that electricity was not the source of the problems.

Defendant (Consumers) also attempts to support its position by arguing that plaintiffs (us) continued to operate their dairy farm for one and a half years after learning of the electrical problems. However, it is unreasonable to expect that plaintiffs (us) would be able to stop farming, shut down their business and pack up their dairy herd the moment they learned that defendant (Consumers) had misrepresented that there were no electrical problems on the farm. Accordingly, I would grant leave to appeal.

—WEAVER AND KELLY, JJ., join the statement of CAVANAGH, J.

It would have been an interesting case I said to Mr. Aldrich, who felt very bad about not getting to present our case. The legal part is now over and we have no other recourse to follow. But at least I did not have to sign a gag order that would have kept me from talking about our case or electricity. I will continue to be the loose cannon rolling around the state and the burr under Consumers saddle. One chapter closes another one opens! It is and always has been in God's hands and now we will see where He takes us.

If only we could have gotten that other judge, but at least someone else thought the same things that we had always believed; this gave us validation.

It is hard to put into words how I feel. Disappointed in the court system, where I always thought you were guaranteed your day in court. Disappointed that Consumers uses the court system against the average individual farmers who do not have attorneys on retainer to do their bidding. I feel Consumers uses the Court system to destroy lives and the very values this country was founded to represent.

But as I read the debate that raged over a hundred years ago between Edison and Tesla, I'm not sure the good guy won. And as the result, we have had to contend with the fallout, and the battle still rages on today. When I read the book on the Electrical Wilderness by Marino, it was as if the battle he was waging in the 1970's was the same one we were waging today. Sometimes I wonder if there will ever be a resolution.

December sees us going to Lansing for another hearing at the Public Service Commission. This time it is on the revised version of stray voltage rules. These are the rules that the committee of Farm Bureau, Michigan Milk Producers, and the utility companies. They are having three hearings and I go to testify at the first one. One of my objections is that it is proposed that the Commission can appoint a panel of investigators. I want the farmer to be able to appoint someone. That way the farmer will have someone on his side, to look out for his interests. Farm Bureau had as part of their policy to accept these rules on stray voltage. They had been on the committee setting up the rules. But when we looked at them, they needed some changes. At the Farm

Bureau convention a couple of weeks before the delegates had passed a resolution not to support the rules as had been recommended until they could be looked at again and changes made to them.

Michelle Behrenwald recommended that litigation continue to be an option for parties who want to seek damages for the effects of stray voltage. Martin Hable, a Lapeer attorney, who had represented farmers with stray voltage complaints, suggested technical changes to clarify the meaning of the rules.

Michigan Milk Producers wanted the proposed rules to be used after a utility company and a farmer went through an initial investigation. The Attorney General also submitted several changes they would like to see.

But the one testimony I found the most amusing was a tape entered into the record that had been made by the then Attorney General lead attorney for the stray voltage case several years before. Peter Lark was now the Chairman of the Michigan Public Service Commission. This tape was a radio interview with Mr. Lark in which he described the problems with "stray voltage", how it was affecting dairy farmers in Michigan, and what should be done to correct the issue. What better witness than the Chairman of the PSC. I loved it; it is really hard to deny something when it is on record.

We have to get on with our lives. It is a different life, but we all know life is all about changes and how we handle them. Our youngest daughter is at Michigan State University so we are empty nesters. We have traded a couple of pieces of the property that were sold, so that the heart of the farm is together. Another year draws to a close and I wonder what the next year will bring. So many people think you can just put the past battles on a shelf and joyfully move on with your life. It does not happen that way.

CHAPTER 38

2006

Another year dawns. I'm still working at the elevator in Turner. I love my job. The people I work with and the customers are enjoyable and life has settled into a contented existence. I still miss my cows. I miss the people who came to our farm each day.

Spring brings another growing season Brian does most of the planting on his own. I try to help when I get home, but for the most part he is doing the farming.

May once again brings another Consumers annual meeting to attend and we present our case for upgrading. Brian had come home two different nights from meetings and wanted to know why the lights were dim. Our voltage had gotten down to 110 both nights; yes, we still monitor the electrical system. So he called Consumers and they came out on Thursday afternoon. Of course they could not find any problems and left about 2:00p.m. The annual meeting was in Jackson. This year they had it in one of the meeting rooms upstairs. As we walked up the stairs, there were about twenty people standing around at the top of the stairs. Mr. Joos, the CEO crossed over and shook my hand. "Good morning Mrs. Bellvillle, somehow I thought you'd be here." I said to him, "I'd hate to disappoint you." Then we went into the meeting. It was pretty short and not as many people were there as in the past. Of course, as someone had said the year before, 9:00 a.m. is too early for retired people. It was the same old story. They had sold assets, the Panhandle pipeline from Michigan to Louisiana, to try to pay down debt and what they planned to sell the nuclear plant in Michigan this year.

It didn't look like there were going to be many questions, so I asked mine second, there were only three. I thanked them for listening to me. Last year I had told them how short we are on electricity in Northern Michigan and within three months they started to build a new substation in our area. This new substation will take the load off the northern section of our substation and part of Rose City. Hopefully, this will eventually help our side of the substation if it relieves some of the stress.

Unfortunately, they have encapsulated a dairy farm on all sides with lines and the future will see if it has any effect on that farm. Then I said that I would like to be able to thank them in the future when they upgrade the distribution lines in front of my farm that have been there since the 1930's. The antiquated small lines and the worn out equipment is having a hard time keeping up with 21st century demands. I told him that it was so bad that a woman ironing her clothes can't get the iron thermostat to turn on. I have trouble getting my convection oven to work; the Sears repair man said when we do not get high enough voltage, the fans will not turn on, so it does not work right.

Count on Us is Consumers motto, when Sears had to come out five times this year to repair my dishwasher because the low voltage of 110 volts has ruined another electronic mother board, I can say I count on Sears not Consumers.

Mr. Joos said he knew Consumers had been out to my house and tested but could not find a problem. I almost fell off my chair laughing. Does this mean the CEO is notified of every service call they make? Consumers had left our house at 2:00 p.m. the day before and this is 9:00 a.m. the next day. They must have Mr. Joos on speed dial.

Shortly after this meeting, I received a call from a group in Burton. They live in a subdivision and Consumers wanted to put a high line across the back of their properties. There were a group of trees that would have to be cut down. The property owners were very upset about this development. Consumers had told them that it would cost so much money to place the lines in the ground and wanted the people of the subdivision to pay for it. The people of the subdivision had told Consumers to make the people who were going to benefit from hooking these two substations together pay for the lines. The city of Burton was looking at a resolution making any new construction lines underground.

They came up to visit us, and Vic and Rose Mier and I went with the Mayor of Burton down and met with the county Consumers representative and three young men who worked for Consumers. Every once in a while one of the young men would answer a question, but when the group wanted their phone numbers, the Consumers representative said they could ask him the questions. They asked me to speak, so I went to the front of the room. As I shook hands with the county representative for Consumers I said to him, "When you talk to Mr. Joos tomorrow morning, tell him Nancy Bellville said 'Hi'. I know I have never met you, but I know you know who I am." The look on his face was priceless! He took a seat and his pen never came off the paper until I finished speaking. I told them what it was like working with Consumers.

I said that money did not mean anything to Consumers; they had spent $1,010,000.00 to keep us away from a jury. We had tried to work with Consumers and not had any good results.

As I have said before, I am the loose cannon rolling around the state. I have a story to tell about working with Consumers and I will travel anywhere to make people understand electricity and the harmful effects it can have.

Consumers keeps trying to tell people that there are no lawsuits pending against them. There are at least two that I know of at the present time. One farmer is outside of Lansing. There was a line running between his barn and a corn crib. A few years ago Consumers built a new substation on the other side of US 127 and needed to get transmission lines to it, so they upped the voltage on those lines. Now the farmer cannot touch his buildings without getting a shock for the high voltage running next to his buildings.

The other is a farmer in Allegan County in southern Michigan. He has about 600 cows and is suing Consumers for damage to his cows. Farm Bureau is submitting an Amicus curiae brief at the Court of Appeals, one step closer than ours at the Michigan Supreme Court. Maybe this time, with another case not too long after ours, the Court of Appeals will hear this case. My prayers are with them. Been there, done that so I know the struggle which all this entails. I have talked to them; hopefully, I can lend some moral support. When the farmer asked if I thought he would win,

I could only say, "It is in God's hands."

I asked one of the Farm Bureau board members if they had a hard time deciding to do the Amicus brief and he said "No. They remembered us!" If we can open up those doors, it is worth the heartache. It was worth not having people in our farming community associate with you.

It was worth people judging you because they could not believe you knew what was wrong with your cow, and they could not accept it was caused by electricity.

In August the Public Service Commission approved the revised Stray Voltage rules. The Commission was to approve a revised version of the rules that provide for:

1. A definition of stray voltage consistent with engineering standards

2. Measuring animal contact current

3. Action required to mitigate animal contact current

4. Requesting an investigation

5. Appointment of experts

6. Requesting a contested case hearing and

7. A protocol to evaluate utility contribution to animal contact current.

Life's twists and turns can be very painfully ironic. The first Sunday in October was a gorgeous day. Lots of sunshine. Really warm for a fall day. We had been down to our daughter Dawn's visiting the grand kids, watching them as they played basketball and football. It had rained on and off all day Saturday, so Sunday was really wonderful. The next day we found out that David Aldrich, our attorney, had been out enjoying the day also. He had gone for a drive in Jackson County, home of Consumers corporate offices. He had tried to pass a vehicle, somehow a motorcycle was involved and he went off the road and hit a utility pole and was killed. Isn't it ironic to have someone who fought Consumers over the years die by hitting one of their poles? He was a really nice guy. My thoughts and prayers go to his sons and ex-wife.

Last May, as I was sitting in the Court of Appeals, Mr. Reynolds told the Judges that Consumers had beat David Aldrich on a case called the Benn case. They certainly enjoyed rubbing it in, but Dave said to the Court that he had beaten Consumers a time or two. He humbly pleaded with the Court that he would have been nuts to bring a case in front of them that involved "stray voltage" because he had lost the Benn case. He contended our case was "power quality" and had always been a different case than "stray voltage". He took our case on a contingency fee, so all the hours for five years, he spent on our case he was never paid. He believed in our case that much!

In December, we went again to the Farm Bureau's annual convention. My work is not done. I would like to make some changes to the policy. I present the changes I would like to see to the committee and they take it under advisement. They come up with much more than I asked. It was passed in open session and now the policy reads as follows:

"Stray Voltage" in the past is now "Power Quality and Electrical Pollution" and reads:

Power Quality and electrical pollution are problems affecting farms and farm families. Power quality and electrical pollution can be attributed to a number of potential sources.

We urge all utility companies, including cable television, to improve their maintenance of utility rights-of-way to decrease the possibility of neutral to ground electrical pollution.

We will work with electric suppliers and the Public Service Commission (PSC) to resolve the problems surrounding power quality and electrical pollution issues on farms to ensure that this problem is resolved in a fair and equitable manner for the electrical users.

The stray voltage/electrical pollution standards being approved by the PSC will continue to be monitored. The standards were developed with input from the livestock industry and the Michigan Agriculture Electric Council.

Research is needed to determine specifically where and how poor power quality and electrical pollution affects animals and people.

To protect the health of livestock and humans, electric utilities must only use approved and proven engineering practices that reduce or eliminate pollution neutral to earth voltage.

We will support the development of realistic standards and investigations, when necessary, by a third party to promote an unbiased result.

We urge utility companies to become more efficient by upgrading their electrical distributions system to meet the demands of current electrical utilization and safety standards.

The Farm Bureau purpose is why I'm so pleased with the outcome of this year's convention. The purpose reads:

Farm Bureau is an independent, non-governmental, voluntary organization governed by and representing farm and ranch families united for the purpose of analyzing their problems and formulating action to achieve educational improvement, economic opportunity and social advancement and, thereby, to promote the national well-being. Farm Bureau is local, county, state, national, and international in its scope and influence and is non-partisan, non-sectarian and non-secret in character. Farm Bureau is the voice of agricultural producers at all levels.

Legislators both in the state of Michigan and at the National level read the policy book from Michigan. Because Farm Bureau is the voice of farmers across the state, their policy book is highly relied on for the thoughts and wishes of farmers.

Another year comes to a close. A friend of mine once said that the next year must be better because it can't be worse than the year before. I don't look at it that way any more.

CHAPTER 39

2007

A s the year starts, many things have happened. Wisconsin is stagnating just like Michigan. Beryl's (farmer's in Wisconsin, I have mentioned in previous chapters) did not get anywhere, and it is believed that they are no longer milking cows. Here is a farm that in the 1990's was sixty-fifth in the nation for milk production. They built a new barn to help make things easier for the family and in the end that was the beginning of the end for them and their herd of cows and the way of life they so wanted to keep. But another family won a lawsuit at the Court of Appeals. The Allen Hoffman's also won their lawsuit.

Chris Hardy has written many articles on electricity. He has personal knowledge about what farm families go through. His parents had problems, sold their cows and settled out of court. Life has moved on for many of these people, and yet others are just starting this journey.

Lee Montgomery from Canada called and says that Canada is starting to try to make adjustments on their electrical systems. Shortly after Lee called, Barry Fraser (he, Lee and several others from Canada came to meet with us in the fall of 1999 or 2000) called. They are working on a bill to upgrade their distribution lines in Canada. He is sending me their bill to see if we in the USA can go to our legislators and get the same legislation passed here.

We just got back from Washington, D.C., for the Michigan Farm Bureau Legislative meeting with our Representatives and Senators. The Farm Bill has to be redone in 2007. It runs out and has to be renewed.

Part of the Farm Bill deals with Rural Development, money loaned to rural towns and cities, to build water and sewer treatment plants.

It also deals with internet service. They state that "without high speed internet speed, many rural communities are unable to attract commercial development".

The Deputy to the Chief of Staff to Secretary Mike Johanns spoke to us about the Farm Bill and was surprised when I told we needed to upgrade our electrical infrastructure in the rural area over having internet service. I told him that half of Richland Township where we live is for sale. I told him that we could not continue to milk cows because we could not get enough power to run our motors, so we sold our cows. We would like to put up a grain drying system, but, because of the lack of electricity, we cannot.

In 2000 when we had gone to Washington ahead of the Farm Bureau group and talked to our legislators about the upgrading of our electrical infrastructure, we were the only ones concerned about the future. This time I did not have to bring it up, a couple of young farmers talked about the grid and the antiquated infra-structure. We are making progress!

I talked to John Schendorf. They won at the Court of Appeals so they now have a July 9, 2007, court date with a jury. I think it helped having Michigan Farm Bureau write the amicus brief at that level instead of the Supreme Court as with us. My prayers are with them. It is such a long, hard road to travel. We talked about how lonely that road is, but as he said, the Man upstairs has control over this, and what He wants will happen. We just have to be willing to accept those results. We discussed what will happen next. I told him that most likely Consumers will do one of two things, either appeal the decision to the Michigan Supreme Court or try to settle with them and place a gag order on them. And it will die an unseen death like so many others and the next farm family—and there will be a next one—will be forced to travel the same road unaware of what has come before them and unable to use the lessons that have been learned by others in this process. They have to learn step by step all over again what those before them have dealt with.

We talked about this being a David and Goliath battle and how David had five stones to throw and we both feel we have thrown about three and a half. There are more battles to come and we both like a challenge!

CHAPTER 40

The years have gone by very quickly. It has been eight years since that fateful day in December when Bill Hendricks from Consumers came to our house. Our life has changed, but there is life after cows! I think the prize is being able to roll with the punches. We have a good life; just different. We have learned to fill our hours with other things. We still miss the people that we use to see for thirty-five years. We are still interested in what is happening in an industry that we were so much a part of for so many years. When we go to the Ogemaw Fair and meet some of the people we spent so many years sitting next to in meetings or seminars or showing cattle at the Fair, some still talk to us, others can't look us in the eye. It really is sad that the cloud still hangs over our heads.

I don't blame them nor do we have any thing to be ashamed about. I really am grateful for the people I work with Turner Bean and Grain and the farmers we serve. They are a wonderful bunch! And they keep my life interesting!

I look back to the time in July, 1999, when we lost five cows that week and I said, "God help me. I can't do this alone. I will write a book." The book is coming to a close; it is a story that needed to be told. It is the story of a lot of different people, not just us. As I have talked to all of the people over the years, the names changed, but the story stayed the same, regardless of the state. As one lady told me "The utility company breaks your spirit and you never get it back". This is the story; for all of those people who had to sign gag orders and could not tell others how they were treated and what they had to go through as the events unfolded on their farms.

I remember the feeling the day I talked to the veterinarian from Michigan State University. I asked him to find a disease because otherwise he was sending me down a road I did not want to go.

Without traveling down that road and experiencing all of the hurt and heartache that so many of these people have gone through and are still going through, it would not have been possible for this book to be written. It was a road that we traveled with God at our side.

In 1996 when we built that last barn, we had enough female animals born to raise our herd to 160 cows; we had enough land to cover the feed for that many animals. We had a plan; we would have our short term and intermediate debt paid off by 2007 and if we wanted to slow down we could. How things change!

I have learned that we can't control our destiny, but I have learned to place everything in God's hands and accept what comes our way.

I think back to the day that the four farmers walked into our barn to attend the meeting at Logan in March of 2000. One of them said to me that what we were trying to do about raising public awareness had already been tried before. Contacting the media, having stories in the newspaper, contacting their legislators, having hearings and the suggestions that the committee came up with to implement, all of these things never made things better for those who were dealing with these issues; was he right?

While we have not made as much progress as I would have liked to see happen, I thought like Dave Stetzer. When you proved there was a problem the utilities would have to upgrade those areas. We have made more people aware that electricity can affect the area around them.

People need to look at the distribution lines which may need to have that extra ground wire to return the unused electricity back to the substation; look and see how close to their houses the over head lines are and to where the transmission lines are in reference to their homes.

With the articles in the national magazines, people across the U.S. have become more aware that this is an issue. The national grid needs to be updated. The use of electricity is increasing astronomically each year and the grid that serviced us since its inception in the 1930's can no longer operate efficiently. And in the near future we will face more blackouts and disruption in our electrical service.

The documentary that Rachel and Shawn from Washington, D.C. are making is being submitted to film festivals this August and fall. It has been a bigger project than they ever thought it would become. I hope it helps people understand the enormous issue that faces this country to upgrade the national grid. It will take a State and National policy to overcome the cost of this project.

Another annual Consumers meeting is here, Brian and I go to Jackson for the meeting. It starts at 9:00 a.m. so we have to leave home at 5:00 a.m. to get there on time. After the CEO does his presentation on how well the company is doing, how by selling assets they have lower debt and now are able to pay some dividends, so they show progress from a few years ago. The question time came and once again I addressed the CEO. We are now on a first name basis, "Good morning, Nancy. I thought you might be here."

I said, "Good morning, Mr. Joos. I think this is my seventh meeting, I'm on my 3rd CEO." The whole room thought that was pretty funny. Consumers are considering building a new power plant and I asked them to add on to the Karn-Weadock plant in Bay City so that the increased capacity could come north to us.

But in the Bay City Times, Mr. Joos stated "the company will not build a new power plant unless Michigan lawmakers repeal or revise a 2000 law that lets consumers pick their electricity suppliers."

I'd like to take issue with that point. In the area I live, it would not be beneficial to go to another supplier because the distribution lines would still be Consumers. They were installed in the 1930's and have not been upgraded. The voltage that Consumers supplies us according to their own testing is only 110 volts before we even start to put a load on the system. If Consumers can't supply us with an adequate power supply, why should I believe some other company can do better?

When is the Company going to come into our area and upgrade their lines so we can add a grain drying system? There are more acres for sale or lying idle in Richland Township where dairy farms used to exist. Without upgrading the infrastructure, any foreseeable growth in our area will be stifled.

As the state of Michigan faces its own economic issues, the auto industry, which was our number one industry, is now being replaced with Agriculture. The Company needs to consider Agriculture an industry and give us the same consideration as other industries where they upgrade and monitor the sags, swells, transients and harmonics.

Mr. Joos responded that they really did listen to me and when I had told them about the Ogemaw County Fair being short on power, they had now made the lines to it Primary. That should help with the shortage of power at the Fair. Maybe the lights will stay on this year. He also said he had checked the power in our area and it looked okay.

What else would I expect him to say? I told him I could quit coming to the annual meeting if I saw new, grounded lines in front of my house.

I hope this book is done and published for next year's meeting, so I can present him with a copy.

As my husband Brian said to Bill Hendricks from Consumers on one of his many visits to our farm, "At least I can sleep at night." I think that when the employees think of it as THE COMPANY it relieves them from a personal responsibility for the things they say and the situations that they place farm families in. The sad part is that someone within the Company made the decisions not to correct an issue that they were very much aware of. Some people have said to me "Don't you hate them?" No, I feel sorry for them and disappointed that people can do these things to each other. For the employees of the Company they still collect their pay checks each day. As for the farmers it totally disrupts their lives, their livelihoods as well as places all of it in jeopardy along with the pain it puts on their families. There are a lot of responsibilities placed on the decisions made by some of the upper administrators in the Company, but some day they will have to justify their actions.

I am grateful to all of those people who have taken a stand to get the word out and to keep plugging away at this issue. Even though it is not a popular stand to take, it does have far reaching ramifications that many people are not even aware can affect them.

So where do Brian and I go from here? We will keep farming as long as we want to; we still have over 400 acres to farm. Brian will be sixty-five years old this year, and as long as his health and the will to farm continue, that is what we will do. I will keep working at Turner Bean and Grain as long as they want me. Our youngest daughter Kay will graduate this spring from Michigan State University with a degree in Marketing and has a job in Ohio.

Our oldest daughter Dawn and her husband and four children still farm in southern Michigan. So when we want to see dairy cows, we go visit them. Lori and her husband now have two beautiful little girls in Arlington, Virginia. Andrea and her husband live in New York City and have a little boy, and our son Kevin and his wife live in Connecticut. We don't get to see them as much as we'd like to, but I would like to thank them for all of the support they have given us over the years. Growing up, helping us to build the farm to what it was, and for all the support they gave us as we walked this path. Distance isn't far when you know they care what happens to you even if they can't do a whole lot about it.

Thank you to all of the rest of our families and our friends who stuck by us and didn't judge us but believed in us. For those who had doubts of the issues that we faced, I don't hold any hard feelings against you. When we meet, I can look you in the eye and know that we were good stewards of our animals and of the land that was entrusted to us.

I hope that by reading this story, you will have a better knowledge of what has happened to people you know or people you can sympathize with, how they became involved in an issue that they were not equipped to deal with or understand. How lives, marriages, families, communities were affected, sometimes destroyed, but forever changed! I plan to keep working for a resolution of this issue, keep going to meetings to educate people that there is a problem that not only affects animals but humans, keep going to Consumers annual meetings, keep asking when they will get around to upgrading our area, work on getting legislation to upgrade the national electric grid, but most of all, I would like to make SAFE, (Save Animals From Electricity or Save All From

Electricity), a non-profit organization to educate people that there is a problem out there, it can affect all of us and to be a support group for all of those who find themselves in this battle. This is a story that needs to be told. I feel much honored to have met so many wonderful people. It is a privilege to write this story.

And lastly, we need to remember that God is always with us. He started us on this journey and will continue to lead us where He wants us to go. As I face each day, I keep in my heart the writing on a small stone in my living room, "Our faith in God helps us through whatever comes our way."

I firmly believe that phrase and shall continue on this journey wherever God leads us.

EPILOGUE

The April 25, 2012 issue of the Hoards Dairyman reported that a landmark stray voltage case in Minnesota determined that stray voltage can be a form of trespassing on the farm's property. The case, decided March 19, found the local electric cooperative 100 percent at fault and awarded the farm $750,000, according to the Wright County Journal Press (Minn.) The utility is determining whether or not an appeal is appropriate. This could impact a lot of situations in the future and help farmers across the country who are having problems.

Life is good again. My book has been published and copies are available. The film, "Higher Power", is completed and was first viewed at a film festival in Texas in February, 2012. It will be entered in many more festivals this year. It is up to God as to where we go with these two vehicles to tell the story of what happens to families finding themselves in this situation.

REFERENCES

M any of the references in this book have been cited in the text. The following chapter to chapter listings give additional information about some of these references, and include other major sources.

CHAPTER ONE
1. Argonne News-Published February 12, 1996
2. "HEE HAW" episode

CHAPTER SEVEN
1. Monty Riechard-Purnia Feed Specialist (letter)
2. Dr. Chris Ashworth,Purina Veterinarian,"Article on Bovine Leukemia Virus"
3. National Animal Health Monitoring System Dairy 96 Study

CHAPTER NINE
1. "Zapping of America", author Paul Brodeur
2. The Minnesota Study-Final Report of the Science Advisors to the Minnesota Public Utilities Commission: Research Findings and Recommendations Regarding Claims of Possible Effects of Currents in the Earth on Dairy Cow Health and Milk Productions—July 1998

CHAPTER TEN
1. Dr. Lyle Miller D.V.M. Study on EMF and Sheep
2. "Stray Voltage is a problem you can have even on a well-run farm" Consumers Power
3. "Power Quality Report" from Larry Wallman, Power Quality Services

CHAPTER THIRTEEN
1. Letter from Dan Wyatt—Director of Michigan Department of Agriculture
2. Bay City Times
3. Ogemaw County Herald
4. Paul Harvey News—March 28, 2000

CHAPTER SEVENTEEN
1. Detroit Free Press

CHAPTER NINETEEN
1. Success Farming—May–June 2001—Cheyl Tevis—Farm Issue Editor

CHAPTER TWENTY-THREE
1. Power Quality Primer by Barry Kennedy page 164
2. Consumers Quality Report on Bellville Farm

CHAPTER TWENTY-FIVE
1. Ogemaw County Herald—April 27, 2000 Guest Commentary—Nancy Bellville

CHAPTER TWENTY-SIX
1. Dr. Sander's letter October 12, 1999
2. Phil Durst—Michigan State University Extension letter—November 3, 1999
3. Letter from Dr. Tim Eyth

CHAPTER TWENTY-NINE
1. Bellville Calendars
2. Richard Whale Letter

CHAPTER THIRTY
1. Transcript of Attorney General vs. Consumers Energy Case No. U-11684-Case No.U-139341

CHAPTER THIRTY-TWO
1. Transcript of Brian Bellville and Nancy Bellville d/b/a Nansue Dairy vs. Consumers Energy Company File No. 01-653444-NZ

2. Article on debate between Nicola Tesla and Thomas Edison

3. A World Out of Phase

CHAPTER THIRTY-THREE
1. Farm Act of 1976

CHAPTER THIRTY-FOUR
1. Transcript of Appeals Court August 24, 2004

CHAPTER THIRTY-FIVE
1. Amicus Brief from Michigan Farm Bureau

CHAPTER THIRTY-SIX
1. Transcript of Michigan Supreme Court

CHAPTER THIRTY-SEVEN
1. Public Service Commission rules on "Stray Voltage".

EPILOGUE
1. Hoards Dairyman, April 25.2012 issue, article on stray voltage litigation